31 DAYS OF POWER:
A Simplified Approach to
Everyday Mental Health

Richard L. Taylor, Jr.

31 Days of Power: A Simplified Approach to Everyday Mental Health
Copyright ©2020 Richard L. Taylor, Jr.

ISBN: 978-0-578-82611-0
TaylorMade Empowerment
December 2020

Cover artist: Zion Bloom
Editor: C.A. MacKenzie

Author's Note

Thank you for taking the time to read *31 Days of Power*. I never thought that these 31 days would become a book. What began as a series of videos during Mental Health Awareness Month in May 2019 turned into quite the project, when I thought it would be a great idea to break down some common and a few uncommon conversations around mental health. I also wanted to help people mobilize and find their power through simple, tangible practices they could apply to their everyday life to help their mental health. I decided to do the same thing this past May. But instead of videos, I wanted to have visuals that people could screenshot on their phones and keep as a reminder. The response from those who saw the day-to-day conversations was amazing.

Many people talked about how the content put out for this year's 31 days was super needed and helpful. I did not want to change the flow of the book too much from the conversations that were put out during those 31 days.

The goal of this book is to highlight some of the most important and common areas around mental health. I understand that everybody who reads this will look at it from a different lens. Some of you might struggle or have struggled with some of the mental health issues that will be discussed. For others, maybe you haven't. Maybe you're connected to someone who has struggled. You might even be an individual who doesn't look at mental health issues and struggles and think they are as bad as people say they are.

No matter your situation, I believe this book has something for you. Maybe not every chapter will apply to you, and that's okay. You might not have experienced some of these topics, but it's good to at least be knowledgeable if, God forbid, you find yourself in a situation that could lead to one of these areas of conversation.

We should be proactive rather than reactive. Having the knowledge to combat certain mental health struggles later on won't hurt. I believe that Facebook also creates an opportunity for us to learn to better empathize with individuals we know than those we don't. Just because we might not be struggling with a certain mental health issue doesn't mean we can't be of help to someone who is.

If nothing else, I hope you gain a level of understanding of someone else's struggle that might be foreign to you. There are many conversations around what we can do to help in this work of mental health. I believe that through understanding and empathy, we put ourselves in a position to win. There is so much power in being able to learn from others who struggle differently than we do. One of the things I have been very intentional in letting my audiences know is that we do not need to be a licensed professional to be someone who cares and is moved to action.

The end of each chapter will have a series of questions and a lined page for you to jot down your thoughts and answers from what you've read. I can't guarantee that every question will be for you but still take the time to consider and ponder them. Each chapter will have some practical takeaways that the reader can start practicing immediately. These are not medical or clinical advice; they're simply practices that have been helpful for me and many others who have been open and honest about their mental health journeys. I hope that as we take the time to become consistent in these practices, we will see a greater, more positive change in our mental health and the mental health of those around us.

There's an old African proverb that it takes a village to raise a child. There's more to that proverb; however, I want to stick to this part. The village is us. And we have an opportunity to help raise each other through dark and uncertain times.

Let's learn and walk in freedom together!

Contents

Foreword

When Richard asked me to write the foreword to his next book, without having prior knowledge of the theme, I replied absolutely yes. I was confident this work would be as powerful as his previous publications. Upon reading the book, my thoughts were positively confirmed.

31 Days of Power. Just let that sink in. In my practice as a mental health therapist, I am a strong advocate of what I refer to as "whole self-healing." I describe this as the act of working on one's self in all areas of life that have a direct and/or indirect impact on our mental health. The importance of this level of healing is imperative to understand. I view this commitment to ourselves as truly life-altering.

The overall theme of the book highlights the fact that we all have a mental health and we must become intentional in supporting it in a positive manner. It is important to gain an intimate and personal understanding of what that looks like. Without this intrinsic level of understanding, you are bound to fail at nurturing your mental health. In *31 Days of Power*, Richard discusses examining this through controlling our thoughts and fears, setting realistic expectations of self, and looking at our family history, as well as past and current relationships. Once we learn to navigate presented challenges, stressors, and triggers, we gain increased insight as to how we view our mental capacity to heal and persevere.

What makes Richard so unique is his willingness to whole-heartedly without fear or shame share his past struggles with his mental health to help others. For generations, we have been taught that experiencing challenges with our mental health is a weakness, that we're "crazy," or even that it simply does not exist. Many of us grew up in households where the expectation was to not openly

1

discuss our mental health, but to keep it secret from others and/or try to convince ourselves it would go away if we ignored it.

I am hopeful that we are entering a time when we can encourage our friends, colleagues, children, and family members to talk about how they are feeling and support them in seeking the help they desire. We have gone past the expiration date where we view mental health as a stigma. *31 Days of Power* highlights why recognizing that WE ALL HAVE A MENTAL HEALTH is necessary for our overall wellness.

As a therapist, I witness the negative effects of neglecting our mental health can have on one's life. I would encourage all who read this book to do so with an open mind and a desire to work on the act of "whole self-healing" as it can hold the key to your fundamental happiness. I am in gratitude to be in this field of work, to have an opportunity to work with talented, brave individuals like Richard, and ultimately begin to break the generational curses set before us.

HEALING IS POSSIBLE.

Trish Wyatt, LMSW, CCTP
Psychotherapist

Day 1

We All Have a Mental Health

I remember the first time that I made this statement at a conference during a Q&A session. It was in front of a room of about 200 professionals in various areas in the field of education. When I stated that we all have a mental health, the looks on the faces of the attendees almost made me chuckle—more of a chuckle out of embarrassment as if I'd said the wrong thing. I went one step further to break down the point, following up by saying that this doesn't mean we don't have mental health issues but that every one of us has a brain and with that brain comes all of the issues of the mind.

Just like our physical health, we all have a mental health. The reality is that it's not a bad thing, but so many times it can be treated as if it is. If we ever want to achieve greater heights in helping ourselves and others in the work of mental health, we've got to be able to normalize it. One of the easiest ways I've found to do that is by setting the foundation that neutralizes our biases and judgments around mental health. How we decide to invest in our mental health plays a huge part in what can potentially come from it. When we can look at it from a point of view of each of us possessing a mental health, it does a few different things.

The first is that it normalizes the conversation and pulls back the lid on the stigma around mental health, causing us to take a deeper look at our experiences, traumas, and emotions. The second is that, hopefully, it brings a new level of empathy for those who struggle mentally and emotionally.

With our pride and human nature, it can feel that if we admit to a mental health or struggle with our mental health, we're weak or that it can lead to an exposure of our vulnerability. I don't believe these things to be true if we can take this from the perspective that we are all human, which means we carry flaws and imperfections. Because of this truth, it can be easy to be susceptible to mental health struggles and illnesses, depending on the attack and challenges at hand. Truthfully, you are not alone in this reality.

Many people have not only shown that they have/had a mental health but also struggled at times with the issues that come along with it. Whether they are everyday people we don't know or well-known names we see often, some carry big bank accounts while others don't. No amount of clout, adoration, and material predicate if we have a mental health because it's already there. If anything, they can play a part in the movement of the needle to where our mind is headed. But the point is that everyone in some way, shape, or form struggles. Many don't open their mouths to discuss theirs, but they do. It's for that reason that I want you to be encouraged as we start this 31-day mental health journey together.

We're about to dive deep and be intentional with the investment of our mental health. Before we do this, I want to dismantle judgment and bias that come from conversations around mental health by letting you know that we all have minds and emotions that deserve our love, time, and attention for us to be our best selves. Having a mental health is not a bad thing.

As we navigate through the next 31 days, I want to encourage you to reframe the way you have viewed mental health and many of the issues and conversations around it.

- What are some common misconceptions you carry around mental health?

- How do you view mental health?

- Are there any areas in your life where you've noticed mental health struggles?

- If you had your way, what would freedom mentally and emotionally look like for you?

Day 2

Proactive Approaches for Our Mental Health

Yesterday, we started the *31 Days of Power* by talking about how we all have a mental health. Now that we have that notion settled, we must learn to embrace and implement practical ways for us to invest in our mental health. As you start to reimagine your mental health, I encourage you to take a "proactive" approach moving forward. Many times when we miss the early opportunities to invest in our mental health, we end up on the side of being reactive to problems from our mental challenges later on; typically, having to play some kind of damage control after we have a negative episode or response from a mental health struggle.

One of the greatest encouragements I can give is that when we are proactive in our mental health, we minimize the need to be reactive later on. Let's talk about three practical ways we can be proactive in our mental health today for the journey ahead.

The first thing I encourage you to do is to embrace logical thinking. This is something you will see me bring up a few times in our mental health conversations, but there's a reason for that. Logical thinking is important for our mental health. I'm a firm believer that we all possess the capability to embrace logical thinking before acting on what we feel. I grew up as a young hothead, who was typically speak/react first and ask questions and get the facts later.

As it pertains to our mental health, we cannot take this approach. A lot of what we deal with mentally is connected to some form of feeling, but what we feel isn't always the truth. Feelings can be fickle and have the potential to trick us into a reality that doesn't exist.

The second practice I want to encourage you to embrace is the power of community. As humans, we are relational beings. Whether introverted or extroverted, we have been built for relationships. As someone who has dealt with a ton of issues that led to big mental struggles in the past, I can honestly say that despite some of the darkest times I faced with my depression and suicide attempts, I did my best to remain isolated. Some people wanted to be there, but I carried too much pride to let them in to help. As I reflect, I realize most of the time I was stubborn or too embarrassed to admit needing help.

Whether we feel as if we're going to be a burden or think people don't care, we must remember that community is a gift and it's here for us. There are huge benefits to attempt to have at least one meaningful connection. Sometimes, it's the simple fact that you have a listening ear. Other times, it can be the conversation you need but aren't sure you should have. On big occasions, it can also be the moments that save your life from a greater detriment. Don't feel the need to try to connect with a ton of people but identify one or two you know who will be there for you. The beauty of community is that it doesn't require quantity in numbers but, rather, quality meaningful relationships.

The last practical step I want to give you today is to embrace physical activity. As we talk about the power of the mind, we can't ignore how thoughts can play heavily into our actions. Our thoughts can be easily hijacked when our minds are idle. Embracing physical activity can clear the mind when thoughts run wild. As someone who is an avid supporter of physical activity, I can't stress this enough. This doesn't mean that you have to go out and lift the gym or run a marathon, but take time to disrupt thoughts that could lead you into a mental slump by being active and shift your focus.

These are a few of the practical steps we can take. Some of my favorites, actually. I think why I like them so much and why I hope you use them in your journey today is because they are easy to implement. As we work to frame or reframe our mental health and our approach, it's important to remember that this is a marathon and not a sprint. Implementing these easy steps consistently into your daily life will pay off massively in the long run.

- Have you been as proactive as you would like to be with your mental health?

- Once problems arise, do you think logically, or do your emotions get the best of you?

- Can you identify a few people with whom you can gain deeper relationships as you work to improve your mental health?

- Create a plan to either get out or move around for about 20 minutes today.

Day 3

Combating Thoughts and Feelings of Depression

During my college days, I was very involved with my school's gospel choir and ministry work in general. I could encourage an entire room of people, but after all was said and done, I was still reminded of the massive depression I was going through.

For many of us, depression has shown itself, whether through our lives or to people we're connected to. We hear and see so many celebrities, athletes, and even ministry leaders vocalizing their struggles with depression. Because we've laid the foundation that we all have mental health, this shouldn't come as much of a surprise. While depression might be strong and sometimes even unbearable, we can overcome it. It takes us being knowledgeable and intentional to do so. Let's learn how to fight together with these doable practices.

I can't stress enough the importance of therapy. Early on when I first saw a therapist, I was shocked. My first words were, "I don't need a shrink to evaluate me and tell me that I'm crazy." It wasn't until I was a couple of months into my sessions that I realized my perspective was off as it pertained to the importance of therapy.

Here's the truth. I was able to learn problem-solving skills, which helped me in times when depression pulled me to overreact. I was also able to develop coping strategies and learned I didn't have to let this depression always have its way with me. Therapy helped a lot because it allowed me to examine life experiences to seek out a better future. It wasn't a thing of it trying to tell me that I was crazy but, rather, a skilled person helping me to progress through all of the crazy. This was a great first step in overcoming depression.

As simple as this sounds, I believe it's super effective. An easy way to get a handle on depression in an instant is by keeping a journal. Journaling is great because it helps you to identify patterns, triggers, and warning signs relating to your depression. If you're anything like me, you might feel as if it's a task to write out feelings, but there are great benefits to taking time to journal. Even simply answering the questions at the end of each of the days in this book will help.

One of the greatest ways to overcome any opposition is to learn that opposition and gain a true understanding of how it flows and functions in your personal life. Depression is no exception to that. There are some unique patterns and triggers within yourself that can be championed if you take the time to learn them.

This final practice is something that we have gotten away from but is powerful; that is, practicing ways to serve others. You might think, *But how is this going to help me with my depression?* Studies have shown that people find meaning in serving something larger than themselves. I've gotten a chance to witness this first-hand while experiencing this COVID-19 season.

I stay in a neighborhood that is predominantly senior citizens, many of whom don't want to go out and can use extra help. I've noticed a change in my attitude and approach when I step in and serve. The beauty of serving is that you don't have to force it or search super hard to find an opportunity to do it. We live in a world where everyone around us has something going on, and in moments like this, we can stop and simply ask, "How can I help you today?"

Does this mean that your depression is automatically cured? No. However, small practices done consistently can set you up on the winning side of proactivity. Don't forget, it's about the baby steps being done right and often!

•Have you ever considered therapy? If so, have you gone?

•Don't forget that journaling doesn't have to be a long, drawn-out process. Take time today to simply write out times where you notice the shift in your mood, whether good or bad. And try to be aware of the things that might be triggering the mood swing.

•Take the opportunity today to ask yourself, *How can I serve someone else,* and look for an opportunity to be a blessing to someone!

Day 4

Addressing Your Toxic Traits

I have toxic traits and tendencies. I remember the first time I admitted this. I had to admit this because I realized I was living recklessly because of certain traumas and situations that were taking place in my life. I believe that for many of us this is a struggle, but it doesn't have to be. For us to break past the stigma around addressing our toxic traits, I think it's very important we face the shame that usually lingers around us, admitting that toxicities exist within ourselves.

Truthfully, everybody goes through it at some point, even if it's just a small amount. I'm a firm believer that life circumstances sometimes call us to act in ways that are usually out of character. I remember when I posted this on social media for Day 4 of the *31 Days of Power* back in May, and I was surprised to see how many people were willing to admit it.

If this is you, please don't feel like an oddball or that you are the only one. As we focus on our mental health journey, we must address moments like this. More specifically, we've got to be able to address character traits because they do play a huge part in our mental and emotional health.

Here are a few things you can do to identify your character and to see if you might be holding onto toxic ways. Many reasons lead us into being toxic. With that being said, the first bit of encouragement I want to give you is being okay with taking time to have heart checks.

Heart checks are important because they allow us to look within ourselves and answer hard questions that we might usually overlook or be willing to run away from. When we talk about hardships, the goal is not to prove anything to anyone else. The real question is can you be real with yourself when it comes to things you have dealt with or maybe some admissions or responses you've had that have not been the best.

As you take these moments to reflect, I encourage you to not give in to that urge that will make you feel as if you want to run away from this conversation or run away from addressing these things within yourself.

Even though heart checks can be rough and self-reflection can show ugly ways within us, you're doing yourself a great favor by being able to sift through all of your mess.

As you're going through this time to reflect on yourself, I encourage you to consider the following:

•Are there people who have hurt you?

•Is your heart in pain?

•Do you feel emotionally drained?

•Have you been holding onto things or feelings that you have not been able to let go of?

•Have you been holding onto emotions from circumstances and people you haven't been able to forgive?

•Are you upset or frustrated with yourself and have trouble forgiving yourself?

All of these things are real, and they can shape us in ways that we don't always expect. But I do believe there is a substantial amount of healing when we take time to reflect and simply be honest with ourselves about ourselves.

As I went through this day for the *31 Days of Power* series, a few other questions came with self-reflection that I want to leave you with, as we move through this day. These are very specific to being able to identify whether we have possibly been carrying toxic traits.

I want you to do a few different things. First, take a look at your current friends circle. Has it changed? Have you noticed that your friends are disappearing? One easy way for us to be able to identify whether or not we are carrying something toxic tends to be found in how our relationships are going in different seasons. With us currently being in Covid-19, one of the things I'm hearing many people talk about is how they've been losing friends. It's amazing how in a time like this where I believe we need community more than ever we seem to be lacking it and or losing it.

I know it can be easy for us to place the blame on other people when it comes to why we've lost them, but I think it's a true gift to be able to take time to ask what role we play in the loss of a friendship.

The next thing I want you to consider in self-reflection is identifying whether you find yourself thriving on drama. As we talk about the loss of friendships, one of the common things that tends to surface is an immense amount of drama. Drama usually comes in the form of emotional baggage, emotional draining, or even high anxiety before or after conversations. If this is the case for you, I want you to know there's no judgment. However, I do believe it's important that we get to the bottom of it.

Ask why drama appeals to you. For some, it's the rush and the high; for others, it's simply the environment they grew up in, and it almost feels normal. No matter what it is that causes us to stay connected to drama, we must identify it so we can deal with it and release it.

The last two things I encourage you to look at when trying to figure out if you carry toxic traits is whether you are a constant gossip. Or are you passive-aggressive in your nature and interactions with people? Both of these tend to ruin friendships, relationships with family, and even romantic relationships. If you find yourself relating to any of these, please remember that it does not make you a bad person, but it also doesn't help in your road to becoming your best self. Once again, I would implore you to do the same thing that I suggested earlier, which is getting to the bottom of this and figuring out the appeal or the draw that keeps you connected to these types of personality traits and actions.

Another great thing you can do when it comes to being able to not only identify but overcome toxic traits is to take the time to listen. More specifically, listen to people you know and trust. Being able to take on perspectives from close friends and family members can be very helpful in learning about and overcoming some of your habits that maybe you haven't paid enough attention to.

Let me be very clear as we move forward with this final point. I know how hard it can be to receive constructive criticism and to hear feedback from loved ones or people with whom you have healthy relationships, but there is power in being able to listen to someone who not only loves you but also has your best interest at heart. Please keep in mind that if you willingly engage in a conversation and ask these types of questions, he or she is not trying to attack you or tear you down. Generally, those we consider to be a trusted source want to see the best in us and for us, so even in conversations that might be difficult, a huge level of love and grace still exists within.

Here's my takeaway as you go through this day. Time is not up for you, and you are not a terrible person. I understand that in moments like this we can easily have a fight or flight response because it's very easy to feel as if our characters are under attack or that trying to address negative things within ourselves feels difficult.

You're not a bad person. You're human, which means you tend to make bad decisions and mistakes. Unfortunately, sometimes those bad decisions can be consistent over a longer period. Even then, it's still not too late for you.

I encourage you to take whatever time you need to reflect and take all of this in so you can do two things. The first is being able to heal from whatever has led you into the space. The second is to be able to grow out of the space and do your mental health a favor by making these necessary changes now.

Take time to answer these questions as we close out the chapter:

•Are there toxic traits that you have and want to fix?

•Have you ever had toxic moments that you can honestly say you caused?

•What past experiences might need to be dealt with to let go of toxicity in your life?

Day 5

Recovering Mentally and Emotionally Before Pursuing a Relationship

In much of the work I've done within the mental health field, many of my conversations have talked about the power of community. But there is no community without relationships. I believe we have been created to be relational beings. No matter our personality type, relationships are a part of them. Whether you're an extroverted person like myself who thrives on being around a ton of people and getting energy from so many at one time or if you're more introverted and have a select group of friends around you, studies have shown that we, as humans, are relational beings.

These relationships come in many different forms, but they play such huge roles in our lives. During Mental Health Awareness Month when I posted this particular post about recovering mentally and emotionally before pursuing a relationship, I wasn't too sure what the response would be. To my surprise, most of the people who commented throughout the different social media platforms had the same consensus, which was that this was very helpful.

Since we are relational people, it is easy for us to try to run to relationships of any kind to help us when we might be in a weakened state mentally and emotionally. I briefly talked about this in my fifth book, *The Other Side,* where I urged readers to consider recovering before jumping into another serious relationship. I believe it's important to understand that it's not just about romantic relationships. These can be relationships with friends, family, or associates.

No matter what kind of relationship, one thing I see is how easy it is for us to come into new or old relationships and throw all of our baggage, hurt, pain, and sometimes toxicity on the person we're engaging. Whether we admit it or not, many times we come into the spaces with this unspoken expectation that the person we were engaging with can be our healer or fixer. When this happens, we are setting ourselves up for failure with a false expectation. I have done this in several relationships and did not realize my actions until I was in waist-deep. It's a hard situation and understandably so. If we can be honest, many of us don't want to go through the process of dealing with our mess and trying to discover healing on our own. We also aren't trying to bring hurt and pain to anyone by dragging them into this new relationship.

I want to keep it simple when it comes to the conversation of why I believe it's important that we take the time to heal first before we jump into a new relationship.

Four things were discussed on this particular day of the *31 Days of Power* as it pertains to the reasons why we should take a step back and slow down. The first is what we identify as relationship turbulence. I believe the easiest way to break down relationship turbulence is to simply say that as we get into relationships, we find ourselves in cycles of ups and downs that stretch every ounce of our emotional well-being. You've probably seen it before, whether in your relationship or someone else's. But, usually, things can be good for a while, and then they swing down and back up and they're good again. The highs are very high, and the lows are very low.

Relationship turbulence isn't healthy in any relationship, but it's not healthy when we talk about someone who might be emotionally unstable before even entering into a relationship that will carry this type of burden. Unfortunately, this is a reality for so many, and we usually don't identify it for whatever reason. I think sometimes it's easier to blame the circumstances or problems or situations around us rather than taking a deeper look at ourselves because what we fail to realize is that it's us. I don't want to sound harsh when saying that, but it's the truth. The turbulence usually starts with us, whether something is said or done wrong. Maybe something happened in the new relationship that triggered feelings or thoughts from the old one. These are the moments in situations that call and lead to turbulence, and this is when I want us to be careful and understand how we can be unstable when we're not healed.

It's important to understand that we tend to hang our recovery on our partner, a friend, or a close family member, sometimes even our children, depending upon our situations. Hanging our recovery on a partner can be easy to miss because early on in relationships it's easy to get caught up in the high of the romance or the high of the support if it's coming from a friend or family member. When this happens, we don't realize that over time we let down our guard from the standpoint that maybe we were getting help in our alone time before this person came into our lives. Maybe we're able to see a little bit of a process of healing starting to take place, but as soon as that early romance or support sets in, we have the unfortunate capability of getting lazy. When this happens, we place the rest of our recovery on the back burner.

If we're not placing it on the back burner, we might unknowingly place it on the people we are in relationships with. This is the third point I want you to be mindful of when it comes to reasons why we should seek our wholeness and healing before hopping into the next relationship. As we hang recovery on the partner and start to use them in our healing, we realize they can only do so much, and then usually it starts to frustrate us.

We must remember that these relationships, while they are therapeutic from a standpoint of being able to talk out our problems and receive support, it doesn't replace having a bit of extra professional help from a true step-by-step plan that will lead to healing. We want to be careful to not put people in uncompromising positions that they did not sign up for and had no clue they would be a part of. This level of responsibility falls on us.

This leads me to the fourth and final point, which is that we should be mindful of not diving into a relationship without a true commitment to the healing that we need. Point number four is pretty simple. If we're not careful, we can bring unnecessary pain to the person we've become intimate with. A lot of times, people don't sign up for stuff like this and have no clue what they're getting into, and on the flipside, since they have no clue what they're getting into, those burdens start to weigh heavily on them, which can have an adverse effect on their emotional health. Once this happens, it's very easy for them to struggle mentally and emotionally, whether that comes through the form of anxiety in the relationship because they aren't sure what to expect from the person who brings in the baggage or depression from feelings of hopelessness because they've tried all they can to help and feel as if they're failing you.

No matter what it is, that pain is activated in them and these are problems they have to try to sort out and fix on their own. It's almost like the old saying "Hurt people hurt people." Sometimes the hurt isn't necessarily spread because of a bad or an ugly action. Sometimes it's spread from being in the proximity of somebody else's hurt and pain for too long and not knowing how to handle it or what to do with it.

What can you do when you're tempted to hop into a relationship even though you know you aren't healed from where you were originally?

Here are the few recap answers that I gave for this particular day of the *31 Days of Power*:

The first thing you can do is choose yourself and your healing/wholeness first. Now hear me out. I understand that being by yourself can be hard, but your healing for a lifetime is more important than a temporary height of happiness, especially when we understand that this happiness might be hurt and pain masked as happiness. I believe there are a few powerful things that happen when we take the time to choose our healing first. Obviously, healing is one of them, but beyond healing what we tend to have is better self-awareness.

We get a chance to learn more about ourselves. For example, in the last chapter, I talked about identifying our toxic traits. It's moments like this where we get a chance to grow and discern and learn about ourselves that help us to become whole individuals. Yes, we're going to have to go through some ugly days because, as we know, healing is not always pretty. Many times, our healing comes through some hard self-reflection that causes us to see the worst ugly parts about ourselves. A lot of times, we might get this misconception that the healing is going to be us looking at what the other person might've done or what the situation did to us. The true healing, however, will be able to come when we take it a step further to evaluate ourselves and each of those situations to understand the areas we can improve. This is important because even though we might not be able to control every situation, it allows us an opportunity to remember that we can always control ourselves and how we choose to respond to these situations.

Self-awareness is such a powerful tool when we talk about being able to navigate relationships in the future, no matter what their outcomes might be. I want to encourage you to invest in yourself now so you can be ready to embrace the true love you deserve in the future. A lot of times, we talk about choosing ourselves as we sometimes blindly jump into the next relationship, friendship, situationship, or whatever else. I look at these moments more as choosing our desires rather than choosing ourselves when it comes to what our soul and our mental health need.

You are worthy and deserving of relationships and community and, most importantly, love. The greatest form of love you can show yourself right now for the sake of your mental health and to avoid any further decline would be to choose yourself and the relationship you have with yourself before hopping into the next with someone else.

As we close out the five, take time to look over these few questions. Consider what they mean to you and changes you might want to make in your approach to yourself and the current relationships you're involved in.

- What was your experience when growing up and seeing relationships?

- Have they been positive or negative?

- Do you feel as if you've taken on the traits of how you've seen relationships handled by others that you watched growing up?

- What healing do you need before committing to your next relationship?

Day 6

Overcoming Fear that Leads to Anxiety

No matter how strong we are, fear tends to get the best of us, even if it's just a brief stint. It doesn't matter what we've accomplished in life or how strong we are physically and mentally, we can still be met by fear, and it can wreck shop on whatever we have going on in our lives. In my opinion, this shows no respect for the person. Depending on how long the fear lingers or whatever that "fear of" might be, it can lead us into anxious thoughts. Before we know it, those anxious thoughts become our anxious actions and we respond accordingly.

I am no stranger to this as I remember how fear used to control me and some of the most important areas of my life. The usual area that I tended to encounter fear was during my time playing football in high school. I had all the talent in the world as a young quarterback: big, strong arms; great runner, and full of athleticism. I've never shared this before so bear with me. Even with all of that being said, I was always fearful when it came to lingering questions of whether I was capable of leading. I was scared I wouldn't make the right decision when it came to my reads in the offense. I did not realize at the time that the fear that I dealt with, whether in practice or a game, led me into anxiety.

What used to be fun and easy felt more like a task I wasn't cut out for. Fear can lead to an ugly cycle. Many times, we aren't very good at expressing what we are feeling or what has us fearful. Some of us are super prideful so we won't even admit it. We're just going with the flow of emotions and not taking the time to properly identify what it is we are feeling and/or seeing in these moments.

If you've ever found yourself dealing with fear and you see its link to anxiety within your day-to-day living, I want to leave these thoughts and helpful tools with you as you decide to fight back today. Please remember that as you practice these simple steps that it has to be just that: a consistent practice. You won't see results overnight, and even once you start seeing results, please don't become lazy and allow your early victory to defeat you in the long run. I say this because fear and anxiety tend to lurk around in some capacity, waiting for us to slip up.

Here are a few things that help me when I feel anxiety kicking in produced by fear. The first is taking the time to fact-check every thought or feeling of fear that comes my way. I've been encouraging a lot of my audiences to do this, as well, and I've had great feedback from them when they practice this. The reason why fact-checking your thoughts it's so crucial is because not every intrusive thought is signaling a legitimate reason to worry. In times like this, I think it's important that we clarify what it is we're feeling that leads to anxiety because if we do this, we gain a greater understanding of that area of fear itself. Instead of going off the rails, fact-checking helps us to put a name to what we're seeing and gives us a fighting chance to combat what we're up against. What tends to happen is that we have a realization that we can fight this thing and that it doesn't have to take control of our lives.

Fact-checking can be powerful as a tool of practice because it leads to the second point, which is that fact-checking allows us to re-label what's happening. I'm not sure why, but many times it's easy to get hit with anxiety or negative emotions and the first response can be one of "why is this happening to me?" This type of thinking leads to greater frustration and, of course, this clouds our minds and judgment even more. What I love about being able to re-label our thinking is that it can shift us from a "why is this happening to me" mentality to a "what is this trying to teach me" way of thinking. It also starts to paralyze those fight or flight feelings that so easily show their heads during difficult moments. Those fight or flight feelings can oftentimes fool us into overreacting to what's really happening, so the power in re-labeling thoughts can bring a better perspective and help us to chill out when we might be on the verge of losing ourselves.

For some of us, the feelings of anxiety can come from overcommitting and possibly even underperforming. This next point of practice is just for you; that is, I need you to learn how to start being okay with saying "NO." Do you find yourself overextending projects at work, in school, or in your social circles? If so, this is the perfect time to get comfortable with saying no. Sometimes the fear and anxiety we deal with can be brought on by ourselves because we stretch our bandwidth to obscene lengths. So, of course, it becomes easy to feel completely overwhelmed or even question how good what you are trying to bring to the table will be because you were stretched so thin. This is the perfect time to learn your limitations and understand that you do not have to be the savior for everybody.

Strong friends, listen up! This is important for you as the individual many might be looking up to. This doesn't mean you are unworthy or incapable. It simply means you are human and you deserve to be able to have time and rest, as well. The word "no" might be something that those around you aren't used to hearing from you. However, they will get over it and will appreciate knowing you are around for the long-haul and will be massively productive over a longer period.

If you find yourself being an individual who deals with the social anxiety component, I want to give you a quick nugget I shared for Day 6 on the original *31 Days of Power*: simply be mindful of giving yourself an exit strategy. As someone married to an amazing woman I've taken the time to learn about, I've been educated so much about social anxiety. It's not something I have to deal with as an extrovert, so it can be easy for me to be blind to the reality that this is a legitimate feeling for so many. For those of you who don't deal with social anxiety, that is why I make this point as we talk about the fear that leads to anxiety.

I mentioned in an earlier section of this book that we are relational beings, and even though we get excited about being around friends and commit to an event or an outing, the closer the time nears, we might not want to go. Or maybe we do go, but once we arrive, we find ourselves with enough interaction and are ready to leave. This is where that exit strategy comes into play.

The exit strategy is not difficult. It can be something as simple as driving yourself to the event rather than driving with a group of friends. Essentially, what the exit strategy says is that the more in control you feel, the less anxiety you will have. My takeaway regarding this is to ensure you put yourself in an area where you still have a decent amount of control, and hopefully, this will help you to keep those anxiety levels at a minimum during what is normally a highly stressful time.

My final takeaway point around dealing with anxiety on any level is to engage in productive activities that you enjoy. I can't stress enough how essential this practice is. I know we don't always think about it this way, but productive activities and actions have the power to interrupt our anxious thoughts. This is something I started doing more and more when I noticed a change in my attitude that was usually associated with me being fearful or anxious. Remember that this is not just engaging in any activity but ones that are productive.

Standing on the side of caution with being productive will help you to not open doorways to things that may trap you and negatively play into your mental health later on. Remember that just because it's fine doesn't mean it's productive. Let's remember to engage in activities that will set us up for success. Anxiety does not own you!

Here are a few questions to consider as we wrap up today's conversation:

•What has caused fear and anxiety in your life, past or present?

•Have you struggled with saying no to people when you should have?

•What would it take for you to gain the courage to be comfortable saying no to situations that can lead to fear and anxiety?

•What are some productive things you can do to help you interrupt those anxious thoughts?

Day 7

Dealing with Vicarious Trauma and Secondary Trauma

This topic is something that I believe will be important for all of us to be aware of at one point or another. Maybe you are someone who is currently working in a field where you serve people, with a tendency to listen to their problems. Maybe you are the friend who is a great sounding board and a trusted ear for so many. No matter where you are on the scale, it is easy to be someone who has to deal with vicarious or secondary trauma.

I'll be completely honest with you. I have been doing this work for a while, and it wasn't until maybe two or three years ago when I realized I had fallen victim to this. Many of us do and don't even know it. Those who tend to have lead others or are natural-born helpers.

Adena Bank Lees, LCSW, defines "vicarious trauma" as "indirect trauma that can occur when we are exposed to difficult/disturbing images or stories second-hand" (https://www.psychologytoday.com by author). Initially, this was a form of trauma that you would see a lot of therapists, counselors, social workers, servicemen, women, and even educators deal with, as they tend to work with people who experience some form of trauma. However, with the explosion of technology, this is something all of us get a chance to witness, whether it comes through the form of seeing someone's life being taken on social media, different forms of abuse, or something that has a viewer discretion notation attached to it. The truth is that with today's advances, we are able to not only witness the trauma but also be immediately negatively impacted by seeing trauma. I believe the more we're exposed to it, the more we become desensitized.

When this happens, we carry the weight from the trauma produced by our second-hand experience from whatever the traumatic moment we were exposed to.

There is no set time limit on how long it takes for the exposure of vicarious or secondary trauma to have an impact on our mental health. With that being the case, it's important we pay attention to symptoms early. As I previously stated, mental health is not a one-size-fits-all. I emphasize that in this conversation because what might trigger one of us may not be the trigger for the next; however, there is something there that can affect us as we take in this trauma.

Symptoms include disturbances in sleeping patterns or restlessness. We can become easily startled and very jumpy. We might notice that we are panicking more. Maybe there is trouble concentrating. Many people I have talked to about different types of trauma they have witnessed have mentioned feeling helpless or hopeless. Of course, fear, anxiety, depression, and sadness can be on this list, as well. Depending on the trauma that you have taken in during the secondary role, you could also experience survivors' guilt. This one is not uncommon when you talk about witnessing situations that might be either very close to home or something you might have experienced and were able to overcome and someone else wasn't.

Because we are all triggered by different things when it comes to this type of trauma, I encourage you to do some simple things that will help when you feel overwhelmed. Maybe you re-read the list of potential signs and realize that you, yourself, have been experiencing this. These are the five takeaways I gave for Day 7 of the *31 Days of Power*, and I believe they can be beneficial if we take the time to practice them.

My first bit of encouragement is to ensure you are monitoring your intake. It's crazy that I was typing this while we were a day out from the 2020 United States presidential election. The most common things I saw when scrolling through social media were the varying levels of concern, fear, and conversations from so many people. While it led to some good conversations, I did see the negative effect it had on folks as to the overwhelming amount of fear and worry. When I say "monitor your intake" what I'm specifically talking about is being mindful of your level of compassion fatigue, burnout, and exhaustion.

These are all critical things to look out for. We must be able to monitor our intake on whatever it is that is usually the source of our vicarious or secondary trauma. I say this because sometimes we tend to know something is wrong but can't always trace it back to a source. I want you to take advantage of not only monitoring the intake but tracking down the source of that intake so you can experience some form of freedom that will help reverse what it is you've been feeling.

This will vary for each of us because our source of trauma is different. For example, if you are a professional and your trauma tends to come from the work you are doing, you might initially find it a little more difficult to separate yourself when it comes to monitoring that trauma. I do want to encourage you that you are still capable and able to do so. We can pull away and take a little bit of time to ourselves so that we can be our best selves in the work we do. However, I do understand you might have a job that doesn't require you a lot of time off to be able to do these types of things. Because of that, there are other practices that we can use.

The next practice we can put into action would be taking the time to talk out what we feel. This is crucial for all of us. One of my mentors always tells me that every mentor has a mentor, every therapist should have a therapist, and every leader has a leader who's walked the road he or she is currently on that he or she can lean on. This is important for those of us who find ourselves as individuals who have to take in the trauma, pain, and hurt from others. Maybe you're not that person, though. If not, no worries. Talking out what you feel can come in the form of a few trusted friends who will listen and give you space to vent when necessary. Having someone to talk it out with can also be beneficial when it comes to accountability systems that will not allow you to stay down or stay in those low places.

The next thing I want to encourage you to do is to be mindful of your boundaries. The power of "NO" that was discussed in the last chapter can hold true for this chapter, as well. It's okay to tell yourself "NO" when you need to. This can come through many different forms, such as limiting the number of videos, pictures, posts, or comments you're taking in online. Or maybe you pull away from online groups that aren't serving your mental and emotional health in a positive way. I want to connect this point back to the very first point that I gave you. In that paragraph, I talked about how we should be able to identify the source of our trauma, and I think that as we identify that source, we should commit to setting boundaries around whatever the source of our trauma is.

Be real and honest with yourself when you know you've taken all you can for that period. It might feel weird at first, but remind yourself that setting these boundaries now will help you not to have to dig yourself out of deep, dark mental holes later on.

The next practice I want to give you is tied into the second practice that I already gave you, which is making sure that we are taking the time to be poured back into. I briefly mentioned how important it is for us to be able to talk about what we feel and having sources and people to do that with. But there is another part that goes into that when it comes to our healing moving forward and dealing better with these types of traumas, which is being able to have those individuals who can pour back into us after we have let everything out. This can come from a mentor, therapist, or some type of wise counsel with the capability to help you walk through your experiences and also set a plan in place that will lead and guide you toward your healing.

The final practice point I want to leave you with is to embrace opportunities to be renewed or restored. As we talk about overcoming vicarious/secondary trauma, the best way to steer clear going down those dark holes that they could potentially lead us into is by constantly being renewed. This can happen through faith practices, such as prayer; different forms of self-care; and reading, writing, or listening to different podcasts or informational resources related to our specific area of struggle.

Yes, it's that simple. It doesn't need to be over the top. Simply find something that works well for you and that helps you to stay on the winning side when you know that you have taken in different forms of trauma.

I don't think these forms of trauma will be any easier to avoid as we move into the future, but our investment in ourselves and being able to learn more about our triggers when faced with an over-consumption of others' trauma can help us to be better prepared to properly approach it and overcome!

As we close out today's conversation, please take time to look over these follow-up questions and consider what you can do or need to do in areas that apply:

- Have you unknowingly been dealing with vicarious/secondary trauma?

- Do you have a support system with whom you can talk about your feelings and also be supported and poured into?

- Are there any self-care practices you could be using that would help you to better deal with the form of trauma you are taking in?

- What would being renewed look like to you as it pertains to this conversation?

Day 8

Faith and Mental Health

This is a conversation that has been taboo for many for too long. I can't speak for the faith journey of anyone else, but I can speak for my own.

Anytime mental health was brought up in these areas around faith, a quick hush-hush usually followed. If by any chance conversations were had, they usually went something like these: "It's a demon," "Just pray about it," "You're not praying hard enough," or "You aren't close enough to God."

These types of words discourage any form of productive conversation that could lead to understanding, empathy, and healing for the person bold enough to admit they are struggling with some form of mental health.

I was no different in this regard. I was too afraid to say anything after hearing these comments come from a multitude of sources inside the church while I was growing up. I usually get this question a lot from audiences as to why I didn't open up, and this was one of the very reasons. There is an overwhelming amount of fear that tends to linger when seeking mental health support for those brought up in some form of faith. Surprisingly, as I've shared my experience with this, many of the attendees in different seminars and keynotes have expressed the same struggle. I believe this speaks to just how universal this topic of faith and mental health is. Many times we see the same individuals stay within their respective churches or houses of worship for years at a time, never getting the help they need. They put everything on their faith but don't gain an understanding of practices that would help them.

In the spirit of keeping things simple, that is what I want to do with today's conversation. Let's discuss a few simple practices that can help us as we try to navigate the conversation of faith in mental health.

There are several takeaways I want to give you to help you on this journey. It doesn't matter if you are a participating member, faith leader, or just someone who is curious and wants to help. These tools can be effective no matter where you stand in the position of faith.

The first area of practice I believe would be beneficial is to exercise actions that will pair with our prayers for a better mental health and a better life. There's a popular passage of scripture that says prayer without works is dead. I believe this passage takes an even greater truth as we talk about the mental health aspect. This isn't to say that prayer alone isn't effective; however, the fact that it's written that actions help to maximize those prayers should tell us something.

This leads me to the second point, which is that your faith doesn't make you exempt from the mental and emotional attacks, but your faith does help you to exercise your authority. As we talk about prayer, different forms of spiritual investment, and identity through our faith, we actively exercise our authority to fight back against what we are dealing with. None of us are perfect, nor will we ever be. It's that understanding that we might not be exempt from being affected at a given time by a mental or emotional battle, but having something like our faith system in place can help us to exercise the power in what we say we believe.

The next point is especially important for those who sit in positions of opportunity or decision-making areas, which is to be mindful to connect individuals in your congregation to the resources that are available for mental health help. A lot of times in the past and even in current conversations, I hear individuals mention that as soon as the topic of mental health was brought up, it was typically just a quick prayer in the laying of hands. I'm not saying that this is ineffective; however, sometimes people genuinely need practical studies and resources that can help them to have a greater understanding of their mental and emotional health.

This leads to the next takeaway point. It's important for us to make sure we are learning the basic signs of mental illness and gaining a greater sense of empathy toward those who might be struggling within our circle or congregations. This leads me to another point that I think is helpful, which is that understanding the testimonies of overcoming mental health issues do matter. Many churches and houses of worship tend to have some type of testimony time or reflection time to share. This would be a great space for us to be able to allow others to have a sense of liberation by knowing they are connected to other individuals under the same roof who have also struggled but have overcome.

The next takeaway is the importance of educating our communities and congregations. But before we do this, I think it's important we equip key members within our congregations who can do basic mental health training to bridge the gap for members who open up with their struggles. Equipping key members will also come in handy when it comes time to educate our communities in congregations. They can also serve as advocates to usher in the needed resources and help within their communities.

As we take the time to educate those we are serving, it's important to remember that we have resources in teams of people that are there for us, as well. I'd encourage you to invite local mental health experts, including those who have experienced mental illnesses, to speak with your congregation or at community gatherings and small groups.

This helps not only to normalize the conversation for mental health within your congregation, but it also has a ripple effect when it comes to your congregation members being able to take that same knowledge and resources and sharing it with their close circles, their families, and anyone else they're connected to who might be struggling in silence. This will also be a great tool to help take some pressure off of our faith leaders who might not have the bandwidth or know-how when it comes to the overwhelming amount of demand from members who struggle with mental health.

I usually hear people talk about how the church has to be better and do better, specifically around mental health and being able to help those who need it. I've even heard faith leaders admit they have failed in these areas. With both of those statements in mind, I truly do feel we are at a great crossroad of opportunity to make needed changes to be a better service to our faith communities.

Before I close, I want to leave a quick note to those readers who experience themselves being triggered by past experiences around faith and mental health. I'm so sorry you've been hurt by people and, perhaps, by their lack of knowledge or concern. I know this can push the needle in the wrong direction for us mentally, emotionally, and spiritually. While I can't change the past, I can let you know that I firmly believe that God still loves you and desires a relationship with you despite what people might have done. Please know you are still at dawn and special in God's eyes.

Congrats on closing out another day in this mental health journey.

Once time permits, look up today's questions and take time to reflect and build for your personal growth.

•Have you had negative experiences when it comes to faith and mental health? If so, how have they affected you?

•What would it look like for you to be a part of bringing in resources for those who need it mentally and emotionally?

•If you've had a negative experience as it pertains to the conversation of mental health and faith, would you be willing to give things another try?

Day 9

Overcoming the Fear of Relapse

In one of my earlier books, *The Other Side,* I talked a lot about the crippling fear that comes with the thought of potentially relapsing. I know how difficult it can be for us to put in so much hard work to overcome a certain area in our lives only to slip up and face that very thing again. And from those slips and falls, anxiety can easily settle in and our mind can lie to us, causing us to think that we are on a downward spiral and getting ready to open the door to relapse. The crazy part is that sometimes it doesn't even take much for us to fall. We can be doing so good in life and progressing at a high rate but still be haunted by the thought, *How long before this hot streak ends?*

It feels kind of crazy, but simply having that thought can lead us into surrendering our hot streak and giving in to the opportunity to fall even though we were doing well. I know others might not always show empathy, but if we can be real, this is something all of us deal with at some point, no matter how big or small the struggle we're dealing with. Some of us are good at catching it early and trying to make changes; others, not so much. Once we set up a streak of making bad decisions after that one slip up, we tell ourselves that we have relapsed. When this happens, feelings of failure can kick in and lead to immense sadness or even depression.

In our relapse, it's easy to feel guilty, and when we do this, we become defensive and easily offended, especially around those who know us well and care for us. We still try to put on a good front, but we're struggling inside. I know this because I've lived it.

I've shared in the past about my struggle early on trying to overcome bulimia. There were times I did well making the right food choices and feeling good. Other times weren't that good, being easily discouraged after a cheat meal because I was fearful of what the scale would say. Finding my value in a number on the scale kept pushing me to a lifestyle I didn't want but was completely unaware of how to overcome it. It caused me so much frustration and anger because I felt I couldn't beat it.

Overcoming the potential to relapse can be hard for many of us when it comes to whatever it is we're afraid of relapsing into, whether it's a relationship we didn't need to be a part of or old habits we dropped but still seem appealing at times. I know this thing is real, and I want to help you today as you pick up and get on the road to redemption.

There are some simple practices we can put into place that will help us today. Please remember that as we go through these practices, we understand that we only truly see the full benefit of them by being consistent and making these practices a priority.

The first one, which I think helps to lay a solid foundation, is to make sure you do not view relapse as a failure. When we do this, we give ourselves a losing chance, God forbid we fall into a space of relapse. When we claim failure, it's a lot easier to stay down in what we have deemed as a failure. It becomes our mantra, unfortunately.

Think about it. Have you ever watched a movie where somebody tries to motivate the main character into getting themselves back together? Typically, the first thing we hear is something along the lines of "But I failed." I believe this speaks to not only how we think but how we respond when we believe we have failed.

My first point for you is to reframe the relapse. Did you really fail? Or was it a moment of weakness and you just made a bad decision?

I want to encourage you to add a new level of perspective to your struggles. No, this does not mean that we are excusing our struggles, but what it does is give us a mental capacity to show ourselves some grace when it comes to not beating ourselves down after we fall. By taking the time to evaluate the situation and what triggered us, we are gaining knowledge on exactly where we slipped up and how to be better prepared next time. Remember that failure and fear work hand-in-hand and can be super powerful if we give them authority and power over our lives.

Remind yourself of what you have already overcome. I can't stress how powerful this concept and practice are. I get it, though. Many times we place our accomplishments and the things that we've overcome in our rearview. What if we change that, however? As a banner of motivation to keep going, what if we remind ourselves what we've accomplished? I'm not saying to do this when we feel that relapse lurks but, rather, having this as a daily practice that we use to keep ourselves strong in our hope and faith.

Two questions are important to ask ourselves when we try to get to the bottom of what causes us to relapse. The first is, "Could more healing be needed in those areas?" The second is, "Are we still connected to things that trigger us into relapsing?"

Be real with no one but yourself when you answer those questions. If you can do that, you would be setting yourself up to have a better chance, gaining freedom and overcoming whatever it is that might be causing you to feel like you want to go backward.

The next practice I want to give you is to practice self-care. The reason why this concept is so important when we talk about relapse is that many times we tend to fall victim to our struggles because we have not taken the time to be as in tune with ourselves as we need to be. The practice of self-care and taking time to unplug cause us to have to spend time with ourselves and become more aware. I'm not going to give you a guideline for what your self-care should be, but I will say in all that you do ensure your self-care is productive and is leading you closer to freedom. We tend to self-care our way into traps that serve us no good purpose whatsoever.

This leads me to the next takeaway: make sure you avoid tempting situations. It's like the old saying "Everything that glitters isn't gold." We can see a lot of hard work go down the drain from a single moment of temptation. When we take our eyes off of ourselves and what we're doing or supposed to be doing, they usually land on something that we have no business being a part of. Let's ensure we're doing ourselves a favor by challenging temptation with this one simple thought: *Does this thing I am thinking about giving myself deserve any part of me?* And if that's not enough follow up, ask the question, "Am I aware of all of the potential repercussions that come from engaging in the situation that is trying to tempt me?"

There's something about our honesty that helps us to get a grip and easily shake our head and say, "No, you do not serve me any purpose besides potential demise."

The next point is to make sure you are creating a healthy schedule. I think it's important to point out that even in creating a healthy schedule, we want to ensure we are being mindful to adjust and adapt our scheduling when needed. Just because we create a healthy schedule does not mean things will be perfect. However, what it does mean is that we have something set in place that will, at least, keep us on track and focused. Healthy schedules come in handy when we find ourselves being idle. Maybe you've got a little extra time on your hands today or a meeting ended early or a class ended early. These little gaps are when we tend to find ourselves giving into old things that don't deserve us anymore simply because are bored. If creating a healthy schedule is what you need to do, then do it. It's only helping you.

My next point of encouragement is to ensure you are not becoming complacent. This is more of a self-check/heart-check type of thing. A lot of time, we can be doing well as I mentioned earlier in this chapter, but sometimes when we do well, we allow our victory to defeat us. If we can be honest, sometimes we get a little cocky in our progress, and those are the moments when we don't see the open door for an opportunity to relapse.

Stay on guard; don't get too full of yourself or ahead of yourself. Make sure you are taking time to practice that self-awareness that will help identify your current situation and, more importantly, your own heart.

Day 10

Downtime for Your Brain Health

This year, like every previous year, has been a grind. However, 2020 has brought challenges. I don't think any of us expected to experience what we have when walking into 2020. There have been so many crazy and sporadic changes in such a short time. Of course, this causes us to have to adjust and try to figure things out.

We've seen job loss. We've seen people forced to become creative. We have been grinding so hard just to survive, whether through school, work, our family, and everything in between.

I've heard comments and complaints from people about how hard it is to find time to rest even though the vast majority of us have been quarantined for months.

The constant pressure to try to ensure we are staying ahead of the curve hasn't gotten any easier. This has impacted our mental and emotional health. With so much anxiety and worry about the future and what things will look like, it has caused us to go into flight or fight mode, sometimes unknowingly.

Today, I want to help you get out of that with a simple talk about how important downtime is for the health of our brain and body. For many of us, we know that it's important, but maybe we'd like the fundamental understanding of just how effective it is.

Let's go through these few quick takeaways that we can start practicing today in our own lives.

The first is to sleep. No brainer, right? I'm certain some of you just read that and thought, *Oh wow, that's easy.* However, it's not as easy for some as it is for others. Depending on our current circumstances, it can be hard to sleep because our brains are so wired and maybe we have a ton going on mentally at the time. Whether sleep is easy for you or not, I want to encourage you not only to sleep but to get the recommended amount of sleep for your body to function at its best.

Sleep does several things. The first is that it provides a needed reset, physically and mentally. When we have the opportunity to reset, we are giving ourselves a chance to approach the next day and our future with a different perspective.

The next thing sleep does for us is to provide fresh ideas. At times, we tend to try to tough it out or push through, and there are moments when we might need to close our eyes for a few minutes.

Here's what I want you to remember in those times where you think, *Oh, I can just push it a little further and everything will be okay.* Fresh ideas won't flow from a clouded mind. You need to be renewed so you can continue to be your best self in whatever task you are trying to tackle.

For the last seven or eight years, the term "sleep is for suckers" has become a mantra for so many. I, for a certain period, started to believe that, thinking I needed to stay up and "keep on the grind," not realizing I wasn't getting much accomplished by simply staying up.

This leads me to the next takeaway point for today, which is that you can grind yourself into an early grave. This is an unfortunate truth, but the truth, nonetheless. Constantly working hard or always trying to find something to do while neglecting downtime wears down our bodies. I do understand it, though. A lot of times self-care and pacing ourselves get lost when we are on that constant grind trying to figure it all out.

As we have in some of the recent chapters and as we will later, this is one of those heart check moments. We have to do a better job of making sure that we are shutting down things and developing a good relationship with our sleeping patterns. You will be grinding for nothing if you aren't physically here to complete the work you were created to do.

I feel this is a great segue into the next point, which is that you are not losing your place just because you take time to pull away from whatever it is you're grinding toward. I've worked with a ton of students and professionals who are like that, who tend to think that taking time to reset and step away from the work will cause them to lose out on the progress they have gained so far. It doesn't help that our life culture tends to push this notion a lot. For many, it's almost like an unspoken rule, so we keep our heads down while slipping into burnout. I'm here to let you know that this does not have to be the case. Taking time away will allow you to be better in the areas that you're working in. It will also help you to be better with the people you're working with or for. My concern for those of us who are constantly on the grind is losing everything because we never chose to take the time to pull away and take care of ourselves.

There are a few more physical benefits of taking downtime. For example, it allows our bodies and our brains to have better blood flow. As I'm having these conversations about grinding ourselves into early graves, let's break that down a little more to gain an understanding. Typically, we see the early graves because we aren't listening to our bodies, but being able to sit and relax help provide more blood flow to our muscles and alleviate what could end up being physical ailments later on. Believe it or not, the proper amount of rest can also help you when it comes to gaining a better metabolism, which of course, will help us when it comes to allowing our bodies to burn and be fueled.

Rest can also help us when it comes to having more energy and helping us with our memories. I can't stress how critical this is. As someone who tends to work a lot and has a phenomenal memory, the longer I'm working without rest, the easier it is to get foggy or forget small details. If you are a creative of any sort, you want to heed this point because you will get your best ideas and results after your mind has been restored.

Finally, being able to have downtime for your mental health can also help when it comes to relieving tension and stress. We carry so much of these and don't even realize it. Once again, when all we know is to work hard, keep our heads down, and grind, we are allowing these issues to show their heads. Sometimes, we even question why we may feel a certain way as we're working and don't even realize the culprit is us. Let's make sure that even though we have deadlines to meet and work to finish, we take a little bit of time out of each of our days to rest when we can so we can cut out distractions that might be in our way. Most importantly, let's ensure we are giving our bodies and ourselves a chance to sleep.

This life we live is not a race. It truly is a marathon, so my final takeaway point will cover everything that we've talked about. Please learn how to pace yourself. Everything in this life that is for you is all ready for you. Do not discredit the work you've done already, thinking that you've got to continue to work yourself into the ground. Everything you do is an act of sewing a seed that will blossom for you at some point.

Why am I stressing this? Because if you can learn to look at it from this umbrella, I believe it can help you to understand that good things are already coming your way and that it is okay for you to take time to step away from responsibilities and demands. You deserve to be able to live a long, happy, and fruitful life, but the only way you can do that and do it effectively is by gaining an understanding that rest is important for you, mentally and physically.

After you understand this importance, it is time to put these practices into action in your life so you can reap the benefits.

• Do you find yourself overworking?

• Do you find yourself dealing with a lot of stress and tension?

• How would you rate your sleep schedule and downtime away from your work on a scale from 1 to 10?

• What changes can you make that would be beneficial for your mental and physical health?

Day 11

Effective Ways to Help in Suicide Prevention

During May, I dedicated an entire week's worth of conversations to suicide, suicide prevention, and gaining a deeper understanding of ways we could help when it comes to prevention. Over the next few days of reading, you will be stepping into a few different topics around suicide and prevention. I hope that as you read through each of these topics, you either find the hope you need when it comes to dealing with your struggle with suicide or gain a greater understanding that can lead to you having more empathy and helping those who struggle with suicide.

Today, we start by talking about effective ways to help in suicide prevention.

Throughout 2020, I have been very intentional with the audiences I've been working with as conversations of suicide and prevention tend to be a more common topic. Obviously, being in the middle of what most would consider a global pandemic, the conversation around suicide is growing. Just recently, Mental Health of America released its 2021 State of Mental Health where their data and research show that suicidal ideation since the start of Covid-19 has gone up 0.15% or about 460,000 people. This is no chump change when we talk about the numbers. Truthfully, what scares me even more is that this was only from individuals bold enough to admit this during the study.

One of the things I've been super adamant about with the conversation of suicide prevention is that I am a firm believer that prevention happens early and often. What do I mean by this? Talking about wanting to help in preventing suicides doesn't start when things are at an individual's worst. Yes, we do see heroic moments of prevention when someone stops a person from jumping over a ledge or throwing himself or herself in front of a train, or someone trying to take his or her life by another means; however, these are rare.

We should focus on what is taking place or not taking place in those in-between moments. Prevention comes in the form of leaning in and being more intentional with people during the in-between time or when they first open up about what they're struggling with, or the systems we create within work environments or friends circles or in our day-to-day interactions with folks we know and don't know.

If we can dive deeper into the power of community and learn to understand our roles in people's lives, I truly feel there could be a shift in the value that others feel, which would allow them to realize their worth. This starts through actions of love and not just telling people how loving they are. We have a unique opportunity to put in place simple and practical approaches to help others.

As someone who was suicidal for about 10 years, I used to wish people would see me in those dark moments and not run away or use my weakness and vulnerability against me. We can be different.

My work around the country, specifically with college-age students, has allowed me to develop great relationships with counseling departments from different universities. It also allowed me to connect with some amazing mental health professionals and experts.

One of the common themes I hear from other mental health professionals is that the demand for help sometimes outweighs the capacity in which they can supply the help. This has led me on a personal journey to take a deeper look into seeing what a community-based approach to mental health help could look like. This is a strong start.

The first point I want to give you regarding effective intervention is that suicidal thoughts and feelings aren't a one-size-fits-all. I say this because when we take the time to understand this, we realize we have more of a responsibility in being aware of those around us. We live in a busy society. Couple that with everything that's taking place with our lives, and it can be easy for us to want to stay in our bubbles or be consumed with our issues and problems and willingly or unwillingly turn a blind eye to another's struggles. I do believe we care, though, and because of that belief, I think it's important for us to simply be reminded to stay connected to the community around us and be intentional in our conversations when we have moments with those we encounter on a daily or weekly basis.

Here are a few things you can do within your sphere of influence, helping on the side of being proactive rather than reactive. The first thing I want to encourage you to do is to talk openly and don't be afraid to ask direct questions, such as "Are you thinking about suicide?" For so long, we treated these types of conversations as taboo and thought they would have a negative effect. But mental health professionals are finally coming to the same conclusion that being direct does not cause folks to want to attempt suicide but rather allows them an opportunity to feel as if they're being heard.

Some of you might be reading this and maybe don't know how to do it, so I don't want you to feel weird about it or be weird about it. There are savvy ways we can do it without potentially pushing the person away. Something as simple as "How are you doing?" and maybe a follow-up question, such as "How are you feeling?" If you don't want to go straight for the jugular, that's okay. Simply being intentional with your questions and actively listening can be a blessing for those in a struggle.

The next helpful practice you can implement if you are in a conversation with someone who might open up about struggling or who you think is struggling is to be calm and speak in a reassuring tone. There's something to be said about feeling safe within conversations. For instance, a parent talking to a child in a reassuring tone about suicide can go a long way when it comes to keeping that thin line of communication open that children can so easily shut down when not feeling safe.

Another helpful tactic in prevention is acknowledging that the feelings of the person expressing suicidal thoughts or feelings are legitimate. I want to be very clear by stating that it doesn't mean what you're feeling is the truth as far as not having a purpose or not being alive. What I'm saying is that they are feeling what they are feeling for a reason and that part is legitimate, and being able to have them open up about those legitimate feelings can help when it comes to getting the right help for them.

Offering support and encouragement is a helpful practice, too. Believe it or not, this goes a long way. I know how it is when we are close to someone who is struggling and not reciprocating when we try to help; however, it does not mean your words or your actions of love fall on deaf ears.

One common thing I've seen and heard while working with different people around the country—and even while experiencing my bouts with suicides—is that in those low moments, people who struggle with suicide tend to reflect on the individuals who showed support and encouragement and even use them as a lifeline when a bad decision can be on the horizon.

I'd also like to encourage those who need to read this that reducing access to lethal means can't help when it comes to suicide prevention. If you are living with someone or are around someone who has admitted they are suicidal, or if you've caught a glimpse of something an individual didn't know about that might have been a sign they were dealing with some form of suicide ideation or other actions, this is for you. Let's make sure we keep objects that can harm out of sight. Reducing access to lethal means can help to reduce the possibility of an accident.

Finally, if you are connected to someone who's opened up to you and you now have their ear and their heart, I encourage you to let them know help is available, they deserve that help, and there is healing in seeking the help of a licensed professional. Some of you reading this might say, "But, Richard, they don't want to talk to anybody or they only trust me with this." I get that, and I'm not saying you should pressure them; however, I am simply saying that as you continue to gain their ear, sew a few seeds now and again. Over time, they realize they've done all they can in their battles with suicide, and as they come to the end of themselves, they have moments—even if it's a small gap—where they are open to receiving outside professional help. Simply put, these will be small reminders in the back of their minds that will be beneficial at the right time.

These are small, simple ways we can help in the immediate, and even though it might not be something you need right now, just know that these are practical and resourceful steps you can come back to if you ever find yourself in the position of having to help someone.

In the next chapter, I will talk about potential warning signs of suicide that will come in handy now that we are taking the time to become more aware and realize we play a part in suicide prevention.

Day 12

Potential Warning Signs of Suicide

Yesterday, we kicked off a good conversation around ways that we can help in suicide prevention. That was just a start as I'm sure you know there are many other things we could do. One of the things I emphasized yesterday was leaning in closer to those we are connected to in an attempt to become better in awareness, which can help lead to prevention.

Awareness is such a powerful tool for advocates who genuinely want to see people stay alive and live their best lives. I believe that awareness, coupled with a good balance of knowledge, can be valuable in our pursuit to help. The knowledge will come through our willingness to take time out of our schedules to learn and do a little bit of research. I understand that research might not be our most favorite activity, but it can save a life.

Today, I want to talk about gaining knowledge of the actual warning signs of suicide. As we go through these, understand that these are not all of them. Even though these signs are super helpful, I do want to point out and remind each of you of something that I stated in the last chapter, which was that suicide and its struggles are not a one-size-fits-all. One person's signs of struggle might look differently from the next. This is why I encourage us to ensure that we're checking ourselves when it comes to being in a deeper, more intentional community with those around us.

I also want to point out that there is an unfortunate truth that sometimes those who struggle with suicide as their reality don't always show signs. There have been many cases of individuals who have taken their lives, and one of the main things you hear was that the person did not show any signs to give cause for them to worry. Please don't let this discourage you, though. The reason I say this is because I believe that our efforts to help in prevention, even when we might not see certain sides with people with whom we're sowing seeds, can be beneficial to those who may never show signs of struggling.

As I stated before, these are not all of the warning signs, but these are some we can be sure to pay particular attention to. I have lived and struggled with a few of these, so I want to be sensitive to anyone who is reading this and feels triggered. This is not an attack for readers who might find themselves struggling. This is our way out. This is our help, and this is what those people closest to us will need to help us.

If you are the individual who found yourself struggling, please know that help is available. Even more than that, you deserve help so you can live your best fruitful life. I'm going to save that conversation for another chapter later in this book.

Here are some signs you can look out for: talk about feeling hopeless, trapped, or alone. This was one of my biggest areas of struggle. The crazy part is that I could never put my finger on it because I was always surrounded by people. As an extroverted person, that is how I've always lived my life. But even though I was around people, I had this overwhelming feeling of hopelessness and being alone that always seemed to linger. Let's make sure we are paying attention when comments like these are made, whether in a serious setting or as a joke. We never truly know.

Another sign you want to be mindful of is when individuals talk about having no reason to go on living. Some folks might use the term "Life feels too hard" or "It feels like things are just too difficult." These are signs, as well.

I also want to encourage us to ensure we are mindful of individuals who might go off on a tangent and give away all of their possessions. They might make out a will even though, from a physical standpoint, they are nowhere close to death. It's a preparation thing. Unfortunately, some of us have seen instances of this when people foretell their demise.

In the last chapter, I talked about making sure to keep lethal means out of the open. The reason I said that is because of this next point, which is that one of the warning signs we might get is individuals who may be searching for means to do personal harm, such as buying a gun. Sometimes you might hear talk about the fascination of lethal means, and this is something we want to pay close attention to.

Sleeping patterns is another thing we should pay attention to. I've worked with parents who have children they worry about, and these are conversations I've brought up more and more. Noticing when someone might be sleeping too much or too little can be an indicator when it comes to warning signs. The same can be said for our dietary habits, as well, when we are either eating too much or too little, resulting in significant weight gain or weight loss.

Overeating was another personal struggle I dealt with. If you've read my story from prior books, I talked about how I gained 170 pounds in about 18 months during college. The crazy part is that I never linked it to my being suicidal. However, as I've grown and done more work in this field, it starts to make more sense.

One of the more common warning signs we tend to see is individuals who engage in reckless behavior. This could come in a multitude of ways, but two of the most common areas are excessive drug use or alcohol consumption. I had a conversation with a mentor who shared a bit of his story, which helped even more to open my eyes to this warning sign.

Before I give this next point, please understand that I realize this is not the case for everybody. As an extrovert who is married to an introvert, I understand how some introverts—and even extroverts at times—need to be away, unplug, and restore. With that said, a warning sign that could use more attention is for people who have a consistent streak of avoiding social interactions with others, those we might deem as loaners and those we've identified as black sheep. I want to take time to talk about this more. This is something common amongst peers in school at different education levels.

The reason I say this is because we tend to see this a lot during our school years with students who don't necessarily fit into the popular cultural status quo, and many times, other students will treat them in that same manner. I encourage a change of action when it comes to identifying those who might be socially closed off or avoiding social interactions altogether; for example, that kid at the lunch table or outside in the playground, or the college student at a party. This is a great opportunity for us to see people for people and to go above and beyond, to treat them differently from what they might be used to.

Rage and revenge can be put on the list, too, along with paying attention to those who show immense amounts of agitation or having dramatic mood swings. These can all be small subtle signs that show their heads much worse later on. Finally, we need to pay attention to those who might talk about suicide as a way out, the ideation, the thoughts of it being a means to an end. These are all important.

As we get ready to close out this chapter, I would like to make sure we are all clear on the fact that warning signs do not necessarily mean a person is suicidal. It's simply to say that if we have suspicions that suicide might be an area of contention in the life of someone we know or with whom we have some type of interaction, we can help to identify whether the suspicions might be giving us some form of an answer. Of course, if we are receiving answers to these signs, this is a great opportunity for us to help in the prevention by speaking up and bridging the gap from hope to help. Let's make sure we are putting our money where our mouths are and, more specifically, where our hearts are so we can do our part to help those who need us!

- Have you been able to identify any of these signs in the past?

- What are some ways you think you'd be able to help early and often in suicide prevention?

- Can you recall a moment when you overlooked a warning sign of a potential mental health struggle?

- How do you want to respond if you ever notice that something might be wrong with someone you know?

Day 13

Potential Signs of High-Functioning Depression and Suicide

Are you the strong friend? Or are you the leader everyone looks up to? Do you find yourself being super active within your company or amongst your classmates? This was me. For a very long time.

As we dive deeper into conversations around prevention and being able to help in our advocacy for better mental health, it's becoming extremely important to make sure we have more intentional conversations around high-functioning depression. The reason why I believe it's important is to better help identify these individuals.

Studies have shown that even though high-functioning depression is similar to major depression, it is a lot harder to identify. You could be standing in front of somebody who has all of the symptoms but looks completely normal. Couple that with the fact that people who tend to struggle with it not only look normal but function normally. They might be individuals who are very active or always around. They are the smiles we see on a day-to-day basis but maybe don't have conversations of depth with them that would show what's under the mask.

Let's stick to the term "mask" for a minute. I talked about this in my book *Love Between My Scars*. In my case, I wore the mask often. At the time, the mask seemed helpful. It allowed me to cover up all of my insecurities and flaws. It allowed me the space to be something on the outside that I wasn't truly feeling on the inside. The mask was a safe space to hide the true hell I was going through mentally. For many of us, we tend to wear a mask and don't even realize it. Masks come in many different forms, such as jobs, titles, labels, and sometimes positions.

I'm not saying that you have high-functioning depression just because you wear a mask. Part of our human nature is to try to present our best selves, so I get it. I'm simply saying that when we wear a mask it can become easier for us to function in dysfunction and think it's okay. If healing is what we seek for ourselves or others, we have to be able to get past the mask and even eradicate the mask that's hiding areas within us that need to be exposed.

Let's jump into potential warning signs for individuals who might be under a mask and functioning well or high but desperately need help.

One of the first things we see in individuals who might be living with high-functioning depression is that they find themselves in this weird position where they always have to prove they need help. I think this point is more important for the advocate right now because maybe there's someone you can think of that usually says, "Oh, you don't need any help because you seem to be fine. You always have it together." Yeah, that person. We must do a better job of allowing people to be people and not having this ridiculous standard set for them to prove themselves when they say they are struggling.

The second sign is that it's easy to feel as if we're faking the funk. When we talk about functioning normally on the outside, many times that can come with a daunting feeling of putting on a good face. It's like a performance. If we can be real, it gets exhausting after a time.

The next warning sign is geared more toward the person who might be suffering from high-functioning depression. Going back to what I stated earlier in this reading, the reality is that high-functioning depression symptoms are similar to major depression. When dealing with high functioning depression, our bad days feel almost unbearable and, normally, we can't figure out why. This is an area we want to be intentional about when taking a deeper look within ourselves. To this point, I also say that another potential sign is that our good days seem pretty normal. During those "good days," we don't usually think, *Wow, this is a good day*, and in hindsight, they seem rather meh.

Another warning sign we need to pay close attention to is our routines, which start to feel exhausting. I truly believe that as we talk about wearing a mask, we can only hold up the façade for so long before it feels as if it's entirely too much work. I believe these are the areas where people who normally see us as finely tuned and well-functioning individuals notice that something is off. During my huge bout with depression when I tried to maintain and continue the routine, there were days when it wasn't just exhaustion but not wanting to do anything. This is a real struggle for so many.

This leads to the next sign, which is that many times we feel differently than how we act. Even though this is the case, this is all we know, and it feels as if we've invested entirely too much into this area to try to change it into anything different. As a result, our brains lie to us and make us feel the only way to move forward is by continuing what we were already doing.

The final potential warning sign is that for many who deal with high-functioning depression, many times self-care feels impossible. If we were given a day off and told to take care of ourselves, most of us wouldn't know what to do. We'd probably struggle simply being with our thoughts.

Here's my final takeaway for this chapter. Strong, charismatic, and outgoing people are human, and they struggle, too. If you are the person who functions well and maybe even functions high but feels empty on the inside, now is a better time than ever to not only reach out for help but to get to the bottom of the root causes that have you in those places.

I lived with this thing for so long, and it almost took my life several times, so please hear my heart when I tell you that this is a burden you do not have to continue to bear by yourself. For those who are unsure if someone they are connected with might be high-functioning, here's my advice: learn to treat people the way you'd want to be treated. You know you are amazing, but you also know there are times when you struggle with things small or large and need help. Treat your active friends, your strong friends, your funny friends, and your friends who seem to have it all together the same way. Let's be intentional, and let's be direct!

•Is high-functioning depression something you've found yourself struggling with?

•Do you have those happy, high-energy friends? If so, do you think this would be a good time to see them beyond the energy they bring to a room?

•What are some ways you could be more present with a friend who is struggling but can't always see?

Day 14

Mental Health, Depression, and Suicide for Pastors/Ministry Leaders

As someone who has grown up in the Christian faith, I, as do many others, look at our pastors and spiritual leaders as invincible. Many times, they have been put on pedestals and held in high regard with high expectations from the people they serve. The men and women who bring such a strong message of hope and a better tomorrow could never struggle, right? This is how many of us have unknowingly approached the idea of a mental health struggle with a faith leader. We wonder how someone so strong, so full of faith could fall to something like depression or suicide.

They are human, and let's take a second to go back to Day 1. We ALL have a mental health! Here's a friendly reminder that titles and positions of power don't make us any less susceptible to potential mental and emotional struggles. For those who might be faith leaders or leaders of any group, today's takeaway points are for you!

Over the last few years, we have witnessed an increase in the number of pastors dying by suicide. From prominent mega-church pastors to pastors with a more intimate congregation, mental health struggles are proving to be an issue that requires support and resources.

I do my best in the most simplistic way to try to bring some kind of help and resourcefulness to this conversation. These are the points that I gave for Day 14 of the *31 Days of Power* series. These were my real emotions and feelings, but I felt these words were needed, and they proved to be helpful as we received positive responses from those who read them.

The first thing to take away from this conversation is that for faith leaders, even though they may be highly anointed, they are still human. This does not mean that it's a bad thing. I believe we all have callings on our lives that will help us reach great levels of impact for others, but that does not make us exempt.

The next point I want to leave you with is that because you are human and because you have a mental health, this means you deserve to be able to have the time to make a consistent investment into your mental health. It is okay that you are not exempt from mental health issues. I know this can be a struggle because the high level of expectation doesn't always come from our congregation or people. A lot of times, the high level of expectation to be perfect or to seem blameless comes from within us. Whether we realize it or not, we are setting ourselves up for failure by holding ourselves to such a high standard and regard. I'm not saying you shouldn't have a great expectation but that the expectation should be realistic.

Many times when those expectations aren't realistic, we feel the weight of everything we're trying to carry and, of course, as we do when we are wearing masks, the weight starts to weigh heavily. That heavy weight will either break us down or crack the very mask that we've been using to cover everything. Because you aren't exempt from dealing with mental health issues, as a faith leader I want you to consider a few things to begin the road to healing.

Is there a safe space for you? This is important to consider because many ministry leaders are concerned with being judged, looking weak, or appearing incapable of leading. Being able to hold space to talk about what you are feeling or going through can go a very long way.

The safe space can come through many different forms, which leads to the next question. Are you connected to your own shepherd or mentor? A huge part of your safe space will come through having someone who can lead you through these tough times. A faith leader who has been where you've been and seen some of the things you've seen can be vital in your journey.

Next, do you have a few trusted friends with whom you can confide with regard to your mental health dealings? Once again, going back to the power of community, it doesn't have to be a ton of people. Just a few solid, trusted sources who can be listening ears and sounding boards when needed. I can't stress enough the importance of being real with yourself. You can read this and gloss over it if you want, but you know yourself better than anyone else, and you have to keep it real with yourself. With that being said, do you need help? If your answer is yes or if you feel you want to be proactive and stay ahead of the curve, please see a therapist. I can't tell you how many times I've had conversations with faith leaders about the perceived "weakness" or "lack of faith" it takes to see a licensed professional, which is simply not true.

If we want to see a change in the mental health of our faith leaders, we have some unlearning and re-learning when it comes to stigmas and myths, and this is a perfect area to start. If we believe that M.D.s are God's gift for our physical health, we need to keep that same energy and fervor for licensed mental health professionals. Please don't let this form of pride lead to an unnecessary fall. Seek out the therapy you need and deserve so you can discuss your burn-out and fatigue issues.

Here are a few final takeaway points I'd like you to consider today:

Reaching out for help doesn't mean you aren't "spiritual enough" or that you're a fraud. God still chooses you, flaws and all. Please don't allow those lies to trick you into thinking otherwise. My next bit of encouragement is that even being a chosen leader, there are choices you have to make to come out better for yourself, your family, and those you serve. This can only happen by dropping the pride, being honest, and letting people in. For many faith leaders, the safe spaces and community of support exist, but I do understand the choice to reach out and be vulnerable isn't always practiced.

You do not have to fight this battle alone! It's not enough for us to be called or chosen if we aren't taking care of ourselves in what we have been called to do as leaders in faith.

These are just a few points to a much larger conversation, but we've got to start somewhere. Talking about it isn't enough, either; we've got to come together and mobilize to get the help we need for our faith leaders. This way, we can ensure they are staying alive and fulfilling God's call on their lives!

•Have you ever found yourself putting a ministry leader on a pedestal?

•What are some improvements you could make to help those who lead you and others?

•Do you believe that more grace can be shown to faith leaders when you realize they are human like the rest of us?

Day 15

Athletes and Mental Health

I've mentioned wearing a mask several times thus far. I believe that, for me, being an athlete was my greatest and most consistent mask that I'll ever wear to hide the pain deep down inside.

During my high school years, I became a stand-out in the sport of football, which also happened to be around the same time my depression and anxiety got worse, and I was full-on suicidal, as well. Athletics was my way of escape, and I wanted to hold onto it for as long as I could because it felt as if it was the only thing that kept me together. I was, by all accounts, an under-confident overachiever. I hid behind the guise of mental toughness and the concept of manning up, as do many athletes today.

We are seeing an increase of athletes opening up about mental health at the highest levels in their sports, such as Kevin Love, DeMar DeRozan, and Dak Prescott. The conversations have been needed because so many athletes tend to live in silence when it comes to having a mental health struggle. Just like the conversation we had about faith leaders and leaders of all types, athletes fall into some of those same mindsets. They feel if they open up about what they're going through, it will make them appear weak or they'll lose their accomplishments. If there's one area we need to normalize in the mental health area, it is amongst athletes.

Just like other professions, they are just that: professions. There are people under those professions, and athletes are no different. Many of us love the sports we participate in, but even with the sport we love, stress and the weight of the world still weigh heavily. I know we tend to identify our athletes as well-tuned machines, but under all of that great ability, they're individuals with feelings and emotions who need help and guidance, as well.

Let's dive into today's points in an attempt to help further to normalize productive mental health for athletes.

When we talk about normalizing mental health with athletes, I think the first thing we must do is reframe our approach to mental toughness. That is because mental toughness means nothing if mental wellness is not at the center. I remember speaking to several athletic groups at Bowling Green State University last year, and this was a heavy point of conversation.

For many, athletes or sports require us to be mentally tough. Mental toughness has usually been described as grit, being able to suck it up, and pushing to limits one didn't know he or she possessed. I'm not against the concept of mental toughness within the sport. It makes total sense. While you are playing, no matter the sport, you have to be tough and push yourself farther than your opponent. My issue typically comes from the fact that many times that same mental toughness we use during the game we try to translate into our personal lives when dealing with stresses. We've got to stop applying the same practices of toughness to areas that require wellness.

This is just my opinion, but I believe that toughness helps us to push past while wellness allows us to dive in. As we dive in, we are able to acknowledge, learn, and invest in our mental health. The idea here is that we cannot be mentally tough and expect to be successful in our mental health if we are not mentally well. I want to reiterate that this notion of wellness is not a weakness, either. We won't be able to tough our way out of everything as athletes, so we must learn or relearn wellness.

The next point is that even as an athlete, you may be elite, but just like everyone else, athletes are still human, which means it's time to address the internal issues that come with being human. These issues come from many different experiences. Some of the athletes I work with have grown up in environments that are high in stress and pressure because their sport requires them to perform with minimal mistakes at all times; i.e., gymnasts. Other athletes I've worked with have grown up in inner cities and experienced a heavy amount of trauma, and that trauma fuels them and drives them in their sport, but they're still haunted by memories. Some of those same athletes are also haunted by the fact that while they are trying to live their dream on campus, their family members are back at home in that same vicinity of trauma and they worry constantly. For all athletes, it's been the added pressure as their skillset is bringing them to the highest level of playing their sport. They've never been there before and don't know how to always manage it.

Then, of course, you have the lives of student athletes, which I believe, get bad raps at times. I know a lot of folks believe that student athletes have it easy because they take easy classes, but many of the ones I've worked with on college campuses go to class, do their work, and try to keep the balance of several practices throughout the day leading up to game day.

These are all issues taking place internally that athletes don't get a chance to talk about or that they may be too afraid to do so. But I want to put this out in the open because I feel by doing so that I can encourage others to address their internal battles.

This leads into the next takeaway point, which is that you are not weak for admitting that you struggle and need help balancing the full plate you carry. I typically remind athletes that they are not immortal. Because we're not immortal, this is all the permission we need to embrace what we deem as a weakness. I mean what I say when I say that community is for everybody, so being able to have people to lean on and reach out to you is a gift that you should not be ashamed of.

My next point for athletes is that you do not have to continue to live with torment or respond in ways that cause you to be misunderstood. Many times when we see athletes in bad lights for decisions they made off the field, we're not always taking a deeper look at the underlying issues that led to that moment or that bad decision. This is why I'm using the term "misunderstood" because there was a buildup to that moment, and a lot of times the buildup starts within our mind before it ever becomes an action. This in no way excuses the behavior that we see with athletes at times like this, but simply to say if healing is the end game, then we have to look deeper. I believe that athletes have a responsibility to be accountable for learning and understanding what leads to certain decisions, and I truly think that it comes by having that mental wellness component there to help them.

Athletes carry a unique set of challenges in their sport, but even more outside of it. Unfortunately, the outside catches the short end of the stick because of the focus usually being around the sport. This must change, and I believe there are two ways this change can happen.

The first is a greater responsibility from coaches and parents. I had a great conversation with the coach of a college soccer team not too long ago, and he told me he was happy that I presented the mental health component to his athletes because it's something he's noticed but wasn't sure how to go about approaching it. As we talked, he mentioned that he wanted to see more of this from coaches throughout the country in whatever sport they were coaching. I appreciated his sentiments on the matter because it showed me that some coaches care and are aware that this is a growing issue. I think we have a great opportunity for coaches and parents to be able to link arms and have these types of real-life conversations when it comes to the athletes who are serving the sports program.

The second and final point is encouraging athletes to seek out therapy. We must keep reminding them that this is not a form of weakness. A therapist isn't someone trying to analyze them for the sake of giving a diagnosis but, rather, getting them to understand that this is where they find true balance. Therapy can help our athletes unpack all of these unique circumstances that they've been taught to put off for so long.

Even how we frame the conversation with our athletes can help, too, by getting them to understand that building mental muscle through therapy is a greater sign of strength.

As we close this chapter, I want to leave with a little bit of encouragement. This is for everybody—athletes and folks who are connected to athletes, whether friends or family. I believe there's something stronger each of us can take from this. I believe we can see athletes whole and sound mentally by helping them find true balance through the simple practices that we discussed in this chapter. We don't have to make it complicated because a lot of the help is there already. We just need the will. I also believe this might increase performance levels during the sport of that respective athlete, simply because they won't be carrying the weight of the personal issues they usually face in silence.

•What are some ways we could be more empathetic with athletes and mental health?

•Many times, athletes are looked at as machines, but what can we do to support them in simply being human?

•Are there athletes in your family or friends circle that you believe you need to be more present with?

Day 16

Productive Ways to Release Pain

We've made it to the halfway point of the *31 Days of Power*. I hope you've been able to learn something even if the subject matter isn't something that affects you. The cool part about being an advocate for mental health is that you get a chance to see perspectives and experiences from individuals who might not be walking in the same shoes. I believe this helps a lot when it comes to being able to empathize and better understand.

With that being said, let's dive into today's conversation. Pain is universal. It comes in many ways and forms. It can be highly unpredictable and sporadic. It's kind of sad to say, but I feel the one thing we can all relate to in this world is pain.

Many people will suggest that pain is a part of life, and I believe it is. I think that we find our power, however, when we figure out our pain and its function in our lives.

We all know that pain plays a heavy toll on our mental and emotional health. We can control how we respond and how we build relationships—even the ways we carry ourselves on a day-to-day basis—so much so that pain causes us to live life on guard, not trusting people and having a pessimistic view of life.

Here are a few helpful tips to help you productively release the pain you might be going through or have experienced.

The first thing that I think will be helpful for us in releasing this pain is to simply acknowledge our pain. Here's the trick, though. Many times, our pride, stubbornness, or denial can keep us oblivious to the fact that we are in pain.

We tend to be so full of ourselves, not wanting to acknowledge pain or holding onto what caused the pain, that we find ourselves in denial.

Do you know someone or have you met people who have talked about issues that have taken place in their lives and their tone would suggest they are still dealing with the pain of that circumstance, but they swear up and down that they are not affected by it anymore? This is an example of that denial that I'm referring to. We've got to be able to let down our pride and stubbornness and admit we are hurting. It's okay to say, "I'm hurting." Does this change the fact that pain happens? Absolutely not. But does this now allow you an opportunity to break down that first wall that's been up for so long? Absolutely!

The beauty is that after the first wall of acknowledgment is broken down, we can move into the second point, which is being able to identify our pain. Being able to get to the root cause of the pain that we are experiencing can help us to clean out the depths of our innermost being. Identifying our pain also helps us to gain a greater understanding of it; specifically, how it works, the way it triggers us, and to better understand how we can respond more favorably. While identifying it is great, we can't stay there, which many people do.

It's sad to say, but a lot of people have already identified the pain and have chosen to accept it or have been too scared to do anything about it. This leads me to the next point.

After we identify our pain, we must start mobilizing efforts to let it go. A powerful way we can do this is by getting our physical bodies in motion. Physical activity can help us release emotion. This can come in the form of activities like dancing, stretching, or going for a brisk walk. Some people find a good release by cleaning. The objective here is to get the body moving.

Movement in this regard is our friend because it not only gets our blood circulating, but it helps when we might want to sit in the midst of that pain. Another easy way for us to release pain is by expressing what we are feeling. Staying quiet and suppressing emotions make it easier for us to explode over a longer period.

I can't begin to tell you how many times I had a blowup because I held onto emotions for so long. When we don't take the approach to express what we're feeling early and often, we set ourselves up for emotional outbursts in the future. Unnecessary arguments or words that should never be said, which can't be taken back, tend to happen. Even though it's pain that fuels those explosive moments because others weren't aware of what was going on, they typically do not view it like that. Let's be better about expressing ourselves early.

As I'm encouraging you to express what you feel, it goes hand-in-hand with the next point, which is being able to talk with a friend. As much as we encourage therapy and seeking professional help, I do understand that we're not going to be able to reach out to our therapist or counselor all the time. I believe this is where the power of our community has a chance to shine. Simply having someone to confide in can do wonders when it comes to having a productive and safe space to release that pain. Sometimes we don't need professional advice but someone close to listen to us. Don't underestimate the power of sharing those feelings with your trusted community.

The next thing I want to encourage you to do is to take time to recognize your triggers. This goes back into one of the first points that I gave you in this chapter, which was being able to identify what brings you pain. When we identify what brings us pain, we are also identifying how that pain affects us. We will always be able to recognize the effects of pain by linking it to its connection with our triggers. In my book *The Other Side,* I talked a lot about how triggers can come in different forms. Sometimes we are triggered by seeing something that reminds us of the cause of our pain. Maybe an environment we were in during those moments of pain that we come across in the present.

These are examples of what can trigger us, so it's important to recognize them because they help us to identify the potential of being triggered. This will also give us a heads up on being proactive and how we choose to respond if we know that the potential to be triggered is present.

Finally, I want to encourage you to take the time to feel your pain but make the commitment to letting it go. Earlier in this chapter, I talked about acknowledging the pain. We cannot acknowledge pain and not expect to feel from that pain. It's inevitable. Because of this, I encourage you to take those moments to feel what you feel. I don't think feeling the pain is bad, because we have to be real about those emotions. But after you have allowed yourself to feel it, there comes a point where you have to let it go. You can't change the past, but you can change the outcome by making a commitment to not allow your pain to control your life.

With all of these tools I've presented to you, I want you to understand that pain can and probably will happen again, but now you know how to manage it and release it. The pain you've experienced or will experience does not own you. It's not stronger than you, and it doesn't have to hang over your head for the rest of your life. You have the power and the choice to productively release the pain.

Take time to look over today's questions and get to know your pain so you can let it go.

•How have you been taught to handle your pain in the past?

•What could be some areas of improvement when dealing with pain?

•What are some pains you would like to release moving forward?

Day 17

Strategies to Help Cope with PTSD

Experiencing traumatic events can take a huge toll on our mental and emotional being. Images and thoughts from these traumatic experiences can linger and haunt us. They can cause bad dreams or leave us uneasy. They can affect the way we approach our day-to-day lives. For the longest time, I only viewed trauma from one lens, which was through violently losing someone in a shootout, drive-by, or another form of violence with a gun.

It wasn't until I worked deeper in the mental health field with an amazing clinician while living in Chicago that I was able to gain a greater understanding of the many facets of trauma. In previous days, I talked about triggers and how everybody's trigger can be different. I believe it's the same for our traumas, as well. What can be a trauma for one person may not be traumatic for the next. This is why I've been encouraging us to take a step back and gain a new level of empathy for those around us.

Depending on the depth of the trauma we have experienced, we can find ourselves dealing with PTSD (post-traumatic stress disorder). PTSD is a disorder where a person has difficulty recovering after experiencing or witnessing a traumatic or terrifying event. PTSD can be interesting because, depending on the severity and the person, the condition may last for a few months or stay with an individual for the rest of his or her life. Some people are haunted by the memories to the extent of having intense emotional and physical reactions.

Studies suggest there are more than three million cases per year of PTSD. This condition tends to lead to other conditions, such as bipolar disorder, clinical depression,

OCD (obsessive-compulsive disorder), anxiety disorder, and a slew of other medical conditions.

It doesn't matter if you are a veteran who served your country or a child who grew up in an abusive home. The trauma and stress that comes from it can have a negative impact on our day-to-day functions. They can even make a life worth living feel like hell.

Today, I want to give you a few simple strategies that can help to cope with PTSD. I've been able to spend a decent amount of time with veterans and had conversations about what has helped them. I've also talked with students who have been diagnosed with PTSD, too, and when it comes to simple day-to-day practices, there seem to be a lot of similarities that people have found helpful.

As a reminder, even if this is not a struggle, please take the time to read over these strategies as they might come in handy at a later date or maybe help someone who needs encouragement.

The first practice that I believe can be helpful is to spend time with people. Once again, power of community. You might be tired of hearing it, but it's the truth. Supportive friends and family can help us fight off the desire to want to isolate. Isolation is common for those who live with PTSD, so do not underestimate spending time with others. As an extrovert who tends to get filled up and recharged when being around people, I can honestly say that it's not just being around people that helps. What I've been able to gather is that being around good supportive people brings a sense of home. It can also cause you to feel love whether you have identified it as that or not.

There's value in being able to be around people who have your best interest at heart. This leads to the next practice, which is learning to embrace support groups.

Having a group that can support from similar experiences can be beneficial. It can also bring about inspiration, specifically from the standpoint that you're able to have a deeper level of relatability. I believe that encouragement of all types is super helpful, but I have noticed how some people get more fired up by learning from individuals who have walked in similar shoes and beat the odds. Support groups can also be beneficial when it comes to expanding your level of knowledge on how to overcome PTSD.

This next practice is a form of exercise known as progressive muscle relaxation. Essentially, it's an exercise that focuses on relaxing the muscles and body in high-stress moments. This practice has become popular for individuals who are trying to reduce tension. The idea behind progressive muscle relaxation is that calmness in our minds is a natural result of physical relaxation. This practice has been known to be one that anybody can pick up and utilize almost immediately

The practice that is probably the most important for many will be therapy. When we talk about the success of an individual over a longer period, you can't talk about that without therapy. Having a trained professional available in your recovery can help you to have long-term success. Beyond just finding a therapist, I encourage you, the reader, to ensure you're taking the time to find the right therapist, which means we've got some work to do.

I've heard a lot of frustration toward therapy from individuals who've dealt with PTSD and other mental conditions. As we dig through these conversations, most of the time it sounded as if the fit with client and therapist wasn't the right one. As a result, I encourage you to research the therapist before you see him or her.

Another great strategy you can use is to educate yourself and others, specifically around PTSD, its functions, and how it works within you. Knowing your struggle and helping others to do the same gives you an advantage toward healthy coping. In my previous books, I talked about how much more prepared we can be if we know the enemy we are facing. In this regard, the enemy would be our PTSD.

When you look at fighters or individuals in lines of strategic work, they typically don't go rushing in headfirst. They get a chance to learn what they're up against. That way, they will have the best chances to be victorious. It's the same way with this conversation of PTSD. Take time to get to know the strategy of the trauma you struggle with. That way, you can create a strategy to combat it.

The next practice is to develop a good relationship with exercising. Physical activity is a proven regulator for your mood and your emotions. I can't tell you how beneficial it's been for me. A lot of people around me originally assumed that my big weight loss was just for the look. Honestly, over the last two to three years, I found exercise helped me way more mentally and emotionally than just physically. It's helped release stress and day-to-day frustrations. It also has provided mental clarity that helps me be productive. I'm not saying you have to do anything crazy, like becoming a CrossFit champion or a marathon runner, but if it happens, it happens. The endgame for this practice is simply to learn how to develop a good relationship with exercise for the sake of keeping your stress levels low.

Finally, I encourage you to keep a journal. Similar to our conversation when we talked about depression earlier in this book, keeping a journal not only releases the stress but also helps to identify our stress patterns. Sometimes we go through stress and can't quite pinpoint where it's coming from because we've been wrestling with it for so long. Being able to write about it will help connect moments or events that increased the stress levels in the first place. It might even come in the form of conversations or interactions with people. When you feel it, write it out. You can start gathering enough data to build yourself up and become successful in fighting back.

For many, PTSD never fully goes away. However, there are a lot of people who have thrived despite the PTSD diagnosis, learning that even though they've dealt with ugly, traumatic circumstances, their lives still have a great purpose. The same can be said for you, and I believe it to be true.

Take time to look over today's questions and reflect on this topic for yourself or someone else.

•Even though PTSD might affect each of us differently, what practices would you like to put in place to help you with yours?

•Has PTSD ever been a struggle for you?

•What changes do you want to make when it comes to dealing with the PTSD that might have tormented you for so long?

•How do you see yourself helping someone who may have PTSD?

Day 18

Entrepreneurship and Mental Health

In today's world, we are seeing massive growth in the field of entrepreneurship. New ideas and inventions seem to pop up left and right. Now more than ever, it seems as if people are taking risks and betting on themselves as they pursue their dreams. There might be a lot of risk when it comes to taking this type of leap, but a ton of reward comes with it, as well. As someone who's been an entrepreneur for a decade, I can attest to the challenges that come along with the process of entrepreneurship.

There have been many times when I wanted to throw in the towel and call it quits. Early on, especially. No matter whose blueprint you follow when it comes to mentorship, behind entrepreneurship the truth is that you will still have to do many of the tedious things on your own. You might have people supporting you and wishing you well, but there are things only learned through the fire. That fire can show its head through many different forms. Most of the time for entrepreneurs, it's trying to get the resources, learning the area they are passionate about, or experiencing financial setbacks. Even more than that, they can find themselves in a weird predicament when it comes to getting people to believe in what they are putting out. And this is not just for those who don't know them, but a lot of times, the internal frustration is from those who know and love us but have yet to offer support.

All of these things and more brewing in this fire can weigh heavily on the mind and emotions of someone in this line of work. Most of it is what happens early on. I believe it's also important to mention how mental health struggles continue even as they start to blossom and thrive in their work. Many times, mental health struggles creep up on thriving entrepreneurs when trying to maintain what they've built. Others find themselves struggling because they are trying to keep creative ideas flowing, as well as the flow of money. Couple that with the fact that they might have employees for whom they feel a certain level of responsibility. Their way of carrying a team can play a part in one's mental health.

Today, we're going to cover things that entrepreneurs can pay close attention to and identify within their mental health that will be able to help them in the long run. These aren't the only areas to pay attention to; however, they tend to be some of the most common from those who are self-employed, no matter the field of work. I think this is good for individuals who might be considering entrepreneurship, as well. Allow this to be a small sample size that you can start using now to help you be better prepared when your time comes to embark upon this journey of entrepreneurship.

The first area that I believe is important for us to make sure we are paying attention to is the area of uncertainty. Uncertainty can come in many different forms. I mentioned entrepreneurs who are just getting started, so for them, it might be questioning whether what they believe in will become something. For others, it might be wondering where their next business opportunity is going to come from. Being an entrepreneur has great highs, but the valleys in between can sometimes be very long.

This is a perfect spot to acknowledge the perception that people tend to have with entrepreneurship. For so long, being able to control your schedule and call your shots has been some of the verbiage that has been marketed the most, and unfortunately, I think people look at that part and don't realize there's so much more that comes along with it.

Entrepreneurs aren't winning all the time. Many times they struggle with an immense amount of questions because while they might post something brilliant on social media, they have been in a drought for months. On the outside, we look at that post and think, *Wow, they're doing something new; this is amazing,* not realizing the post was an attempt to bring in a few dollars simply to pay the bills. This is just one example of something that can lead to uncertainty during the process. The tricky part with uncertainty is that it can lead us into a huge rush of anxiety. Once this happens, we freak out because we feel as if everything is out of control.

That uncertainty causes us to start creating scenarios in our minds that don't exist. When we don't know how to combat uncertainty, it can become easy for an entrepreneur to try anything just to make something work. The issue with this is that it pulls us away from what we're supposed to do because we're being led by pressure and not by passion. If you need to, I encourage you to take a look back over the first few days in this book where we talked about ways to combat anxiety. Those practices would be very helpful in moments of uncertainty.

The next items we must pay attention to when it comes to making sure we are being proactive in our mental health when self-employed are our identities and self-worth. Many times in the field of entrepreneurship, we see identity and self-worth issues based on the productivity or success of our brand or business. At times, I've noticed that people have this tendency to place their self-worth into the very thing that they believe in. I'm not a huge supporter of that. Don't get me wrong. I do understand that our vision and our passion are our babies. We dream it, and we live it to the T, but we still have to be reminded that this dream and passion are only a portion of us. They are not our entire makeup or identity. When we start to treat them as if they are, it can be easy to look at the valley moments of entrepreneurship and punish ourselves because of it. Just because your business isn't moving doesn't mean you are lacking. Just because you're not seeing the numbers that you thought you would see in this season, doesn't mean you are a failure. I believe there is a healthy space within which to separate ourselves from the things we are so passionate about.

Many times, motivational speakers tell listeners that they have to be all in on whatever it is that they are working toward. Some speakers have encouraged us to go without sleep for the sake of success, and there are many other tweetable quotes, as well. While a lot of this sounds good as a form of motivation, the truth is that many times it's not tangible and not conducive for good mental health. My encouragement is balance in all things. Yes, your brand and business may be an extension of you, but it is not where your value and self-worth are.

How you rest is next on our list of things to pay attention to for the sake of our mental health and managing stress. Many times as entrepreneurs, we tend to be sleep-deprived, and there is a lack of emphasis on taking care of ourselves. I've heard many entrepreneurs reference the term "Sleep is for suckers" or "I've got to stay on the grind." Unfortunately, these mindsets have become lifestyles of many entrepreneurs. Once again, while I do understand the concept from a motivational standpoint, it is a lot more counterproductive than we give it credit for, not realizing that denying ourselves sleep can cause issues to our body.

As well, lack of rest doesn't help our thinking to create better within our realm of work. You couple that with an "I've got to stay on the grind" mentality, and it's a set-up for disaster. A lot of times we're choosing the grind over self-care, and the outcome tends to be stress. And this is just one form of it. There are also stresses that come from the daily flow of our work, family issues, and other external factors that we might be connected to. Many of us tend to be very independent and don't ask for help. Adding that in, as well, can show the greatest signs of stress for an individual.

If we can be honest and take the time to identify stress within ourselves, I believe we can reverse the curse and help our bodies and minds to function properly. Stress is one of the leading killers. We, as entrepreneurs, aren't any different. If we're not taking care of ourselves, we could succumb to the same outcome.

The final practice I want you to be able to identify is wearing a mask. No, I'm not talking about masks due to Covid-19. I'm talking about the masks we wear as entrepreneurs when we feel as if we have to show people that we have it all together. Many times, we don't want people to know we're struggling or that we genuinely need help. Sometimes we're trying to put on a good face to prove our doubters or haters wrong so we will always be on guard and always say the right things. That way, we don't get caught slipping. The unfortunate reality is that when we do this we're damaging ourselves more than we know because after so long, we can start to live as if everything is okay even though everything around us is pure chaos. The truth is that entrepreneurship is not a have-it-all-together journey. We will always experience mountains and valleys even as we grow and progress. And there is nothing wrong with that.

While entrepreneurs might be unique in some of their struggles that lead to mental health issues, we are not unique when it comes to the best practices that will help us. I encourage you to look back through some of the earlier chapters to pull those best practices to make the changes you would like to see. I believe we all have something great inside of us when it comes to creating, whether that be a product or a new idea. We deserve to be able to see those things come to fruition, but we won't be able to if we're not taking the time to address our mental health as entrepreneurs and self-employed individuals. You do not have to walk this journey on your own.

Take time to look over today's questions and reflect as needed.

- What are some ways as an entrepreneur that you would like to make a greater investment into your mental health?

- While trying to create amazing content, products, or brands, how are you being intentional about staying afloat with your mental and emotional health?

Day 19

Unhealthy Quotes and Myths about Mental Health in Communities of Color

Growing up, I've heard many different things when it comes to the stigmas associated with mental health. As my work in this field has allowed me to reach people around the globe, I've gotten a chance to talk to people about some of the unhealthy quotes and stigmas they've heard growing up, as well. There were a lot of commonalities for many of us even though we came from different cultures and backgrounds.

Today, we're going to look through some of the most common ones that I've found. I hope these help us to take a deeper look at what we've been taught and figure out what we might need to unlearn.

I briefly discuss this first myth in my book *Love Between My Scars*. It was something I've heard growing up in the black community for so long and never really questioned: that when it came to mental health issues, it was a white person's problem. For a time, it made sense to me, too. When recalling what the representation in the media, movies, and day-to-day life looked like when I was growing up, we weren't seeing people that looked like us having conversations around these topics of mental health. Most of the commercials for a new medicine for mental health related issues that I would see in between news segments or soap operas were usually white people who were cast for the roles.

As I continued to struggle more and more with my mental health, I knew this problem wasn't solely related to white people, but I wasn't sure where to turn to receive the necessary help because I didn't know where black people went for mental health issues. If we're following the premise that we all have a mental health, we understand that this being a white person's problem is simply not true. We can all be affected by it depending on our circumstances, and what triggers it might end up leading to it.

The next myth I want to bust is the idea that our ancestors dealt with worse. Don't get me wrong. Looking back at the trans-Atlantic slave trade, the building of the nation, wars, and other traumas that occurred during their time, they went through a lot. However, my encouragement for this portion of the conversation is not to bring about comparison. Our ancestors did go through so much unjust turmoil & trauma; however, they didn't have resources and couldn't talk about what they were dealing with. Today, we have resources, and we have the ability to talk openly about our feelings. This is a great spot to mention that when we hear people, mostly younger people, open up about their mental health, we have to stop demonizing them with this type of rhetoric.

No one is saying that our ancestors didn't have it bad. When people are bold enough to open up, we must hear their hearts and pause on our brainless responses. Effective healing for people's mental health won't come with a comparison of who had it worse. We are no longer living in a just-shut-up-and-deal-with-it society anymore. Resources are available, and people genuinely want to release their struggles so they can heal. That's not a bad thing, and our responsibility and heart posture should be helping folks to get to that healing. When they open up to you, consider it a gift because, in all honesty, they could've remained quiet and had you looking clueless, God forbid they were to act on what they've been feeling mentally and emotionally. This is an opportunity to take advantage of the signs you're given.

The next myth we need to talk about is parents and the idea that they provide everything a child needs so they have no reason to be depressed. This one is critical and also very dangerous. My work also has brought me into corporate spaces where I might work with parents and answer questions because a lot of my work has me working with middle/high school and college-age students across the country. One of the common things I hear from parents is, "I'm giving my child everything. I just don't understand why they're depressed or anxious."

One of the first things I tell them is that when we talk about mental health issues of any kind, they can't be fixed with material things. We must remember that these are internal battles that require inner healing, not a new toy or car to fix it.

This is in no way throwing shade to the provision that parents give for their children. It has more to do with the reality that if mental and emotional pain is taking place in the minds of our children, it's going to take more relational intentionality and professional help, not just monetary provision.

I'd also like to remind parents reading this that you are doing a great job providing for your children. Just because they may be struggling with mental health issues does not make you any less effective or that you're a failure. Continue to be the best loving parent you can be because I do believe these issues can be overcome in due time.

The next method I use is another one that was discussed briefly in *Love Between My Scars*. When I mention this one in speeches, I usually get a lot of handclaps or "say that" from people in the audience. This is the notion that it's just a demon and you need to pray about it or the idea that you're not praying hard enough and lack closeness to God.

As someone who grew up in the church, it was hard hearing this because it almost felt as if there was no way out. I do believe in the power of prayer and how effective it could be, but our faith teaches us that there is natural work that we must do, as well. Henceforth, the passage "faith without works" is dead. One of the conversations I've been having with faith leaders and their congregations is that you can still have belief in your faith and see a therapist. That is the work part that, when put into action, can help what we're praying for.

There have been many people who have been demonized with this conversation because of those exact words, and they have a lot of hurt and ill feelings toward the church and church people. This is a result of what I discussed in an earlier chapter about faith and mental health. This is why bringing resources into these areas can be helpful. That way, we're putting out the right messaging that will allow people to get the help they need for their mental and emotional health.

The next quote is one I'm pretty sure many of you have heard before, and that is, "What happens in this house, stays in this house." This has done so much damage to so many people who genuinely need or needed the help at a younger age. This quote essentially acted as a wall or a code of silence. It has crippled the tongues of so many who need a perspective or treatment, which is unfortunate because a lot of times the words usually came from a parent or guardian. When this happens, sometimes parents would be watching their children on a steady decline and couldn't figure out for the life of them what was going on.

This leads to another ideology that wasn't helpful, either, which is the notion that no therapist or counselor needs to know our business. I get it. Culturally, things look different for different people.

In 2020 I did an episode on my podcast about why certain cultures might feel this way. For some, it's a matter of social status and having to keep an image. For others, it's viewed as a sign of weakness to admit that someone in the house is struggling. Similar to what we just talked about with the entrepreneurs, we wear masks to try to make it seem as if we have it all together. We do this because we don't want people to view us in a negative light, potentially gossip, or start rumors about us or our families.

I believe we've got to start gaining a new level of perspective as to how we look at therapy. This is not just a sit-down that's a waste of time. This isn't a person who wants to know all of your business and judge you. Truthfully, it's not your business that the mental health professional is concerned about. When you have physical ailments, do you say, "I don't need the doctor to know what's going on with me even though I'm in pain and I want to rid myself of it?" Absolutely not. You research to try to find the best person for the job to help.

We must start treating therapy the same way. Sometimes, we tend to be our own worst enemy, and this is one example of that. Therapists are not in the business of trying to know your business but to help you address and overcome traumas and issues.

We've got to work towards breaking this unhealthy model of not talking about what's going on. The help and the resources are there for you to help you. Let's learn how to start getting over ourselves and our unhealthy learned thought processes toward mental health.

Those are just a few of the unhealthy quotes and myths we hear. There are many more. No matter what it is you've been taught around this that can be identified as being unhealthy, I believe it's important that we look within ourselves to reassess what we've learned and define the learned behaviors that need to be eradicated.

Take time to look over today's questions and reflect as needed. You are a myth buster!

•What is a common misconception that you grew up believing about mental health?

•What is one area or thought that you would like to change within the minds of people when it comes to the truth about mental health?

•How have misconceptions about mental health affected you today?

Day 20

Coping Through Grief

Grief is something that I believe we all go through at some point in our lives. It's typically triggered by a loss of some proportion, whether losing a person we love dearly, a job we thought we'd have forever, or something as simple as a change of environment that we didn't see coming. No matter what it is that triggers us in grief, the grief is tough.

The craziest part about grief is a lot of times we are going through it and don't even realize it. Our thought process might change and we can even act out, but it takes a good amount of awareness to recognize exactly what's happening.

I believe that once we acknowledge and identify what has us grieving, we can move forward to cope and potentially heal. So, today, we're going to focus on some simple practices to cope through grief.

Coping through and trying to find some form of healing does not mean you will forget what it is or who it is you might be grieving, but it does mean you have an opportunity to learn how to live your best life through the grief.

The first practice I want to give you is to remember to be gentle with yourself. I think sometimes when we go through the grieving process we forget we aren't perfect beings. Neither is the process of grieving perfect. This means that each day will look different, and sometimes even moments within the same day can look different, as well. This is why the reminder to be gentle with ourselves is such a powerful tool when it comes to coping and managing grief. When we can take a step back to show ourselves grace, we are doing ourselves a favor by not adding on more weight that can result in stress, anxiety, or even deep bouts of depression.

I want to encourage you to learn to embrace your feelings. The emotions that come with grief are real, and we can't ignore them when they arise. It's easy to turn a blind eye or to try to keep ourselves occupied so we don't worry about whatever it is that has us in this mental state. This is not helpful in the long run, however. This reminds me of the quote that Thanos had in *Avengers Endgame*, when he said, "You could not live with your own failure, and where did that bring you? Back to me." This is how it is when we choose not to embrace what we're feeling.

A lot of times, we can feel things like failure or guilt and do our best to run from them. However, no matter how far we run, we're always brought back to those initial feelings. I want to encourage you to acknowledge what you feel so you can embrace it. I do understand that a lot of times embracing what you feel means having to come to grips with the reality of whatever it is that caused us to grieve. There's typically some kind of pain involved and some hardships, maybe even bad decisions that we must acknowledge. I understand how the weight of that embrace can feel unbearable, but I am a firm believer that the quicker we embrace what we feel and simply just feel it, we can move in the right direction toward our healing.

This leads me to the next practice, which is to identify guilt. As I stated in the previous paragraph, it's not a secret that as we embrace what we feel, there will be a ton of emotions and feelings that come with what we have to face. Guilt usually sits somewhere at the top of that list, whether it's from losing a person we loved dearly and trying to figure out how we survived when they didn't, or losing something super valuable that you haven't been able to stop blaming yourself for because that thing no longer exists in your life.

Guilt can be very sneaky and cunning. A lot of times, it will play on our vulnerabilities, along with the fact that we sometimes aren't thinking straight when we grieve. This is why it's so important for us to identify guilt when it does decide to show itself to us at random times.

Guilt has an interesting way about itself. It can torment us and cripple our forward progress. For this to happen, we typically have to allow guilt an area to rest in our minds and our hearts. So the key, after we identify guilt, is to learn to cut it off by gaining an understanding that it does not deserve space and opportunity to torment you.

The next helpful practice in coping is for us to learn to understand the anger we feel in times of grief. Understanding the anger can help us to dissect what's triggering us. It also helps us to gain a greater sense of control. That sense of control can be beneficial when it comes to not feeling the need to respond to the anger.

As someone who has dealt with anger issues as a child and into young adulthood, I wish I had known then what I know now about not being controlled by anger. Understanding your anger doesn't mean you are giving it a pass, either. It means you are taking the time to learn its functions so you can take your power back from the very anger that sometimes leads you into seeing red and responding accordingly.

Addictions are a very huge part of grief. They can happen quickly as we struggle, and we don't even realize it. A lot of times, they don't start as addictions. We just indulge in certain things now and again, and unfortunately, that now and again can become habitual. Over time, those habitual practices start to feel like a needed part of our daily living.

This is why this next practice is so important in helping us to productively cope with grief. We've got to start identifying doorways that lead to addiction. This practice simply means that we will have to take more time to become self-aware in seasons of grief.

One of the easiest ways for us to identify the doorway is to keep an eye out for those early habits. With grief, you will be presented with opportunities that sometimes seem like coping, but they are not productive for helping you to cope in the right direction forward, so please make sure you ask questions about the things or people you are considering to let into your life.

The next practice we can start putting into action is being willing to talk about what we feel when we can. The key word from that last sentence is "willing." If we're being completely honest when we are struggling, many times we do not feel like doing anything. We lack the willingness to try to do anything because of what we are going through and how heavy it feels on us. Even though we know the community is there for us, we aren't always willing to talk to our community. We remain quiet and struggle on our own when we don't have to.

Even if you don't feel like talking, I need you to understand that finding ways to express your thoughts and emotions can be beneficial. Simply calling or texting a friend or having a face-to-face can go a long way in your recovery and healing. So while I want you to engage in reaching out for help and talking, I also want you to hone in on what might be causing you to not feel willing when hope and help present themselves.

The final practice I want to leave with you is to join a support group. Support groups offer a community of individuals who share similar experiences. I believe that, for those of us who experience grief, this could be a game-changer by being able to sit back and take it all in. Support groups allow you space and an opportunity to be yourself with whatever feelings you're experiencing. You can be vulnerable; you can cry. You can be mad, and most importantly, you can learn, not just by learning the stories of others but also by learning how they found the willingness to fight and live another day. I encourage you to take a leap of faith to give a supportive group an opportunity.

As we wrap up this chapter, I want you to know that you are not alone in your feelings while you grieve. Please don't think that you are. Grief over a longer time-frame can open doorways to a ton of other mental health issues that you don't need to invite into your life. Even with the grief, your best days are still ahead of you.

Take time to look over today's questions and answer them. Reflect when and where needed.

•Has grief affected you anytime in your past?

•In what areas of life are grieving and might want to be honest about and work toward changing?

Day 21

Overcoming Self-Sabotage

Self-sabotage is a phrase we hear often in this 21st century. Many social influencers as well our world's greatest thought leaders talk about it. It is very real and can have damaging effects on our mental health and the way we live our lives.

Many times, we don't even realize we are sabotaging ourselves. Most of the time, self-sabotage can feel like a normal day, or it can feel like normal actions that aren't really normal at all. The definition of sabotage is when we actively or passively take steps to prevent ourselves from reaching our goals.

Interestingly enough, self-sabotage can show its face in any area of our lives. I'm talking about working toward our dreams and goals, at our jobs, social groups, and even relationships with friends or family. Especially in romantic relationships.

There can be many causes for self-sabotage. Here are three that I normally see that gaslight self-sabotaging our own lives. They can show in the form of fear, thinking patterns (overthinking), and our urge to try to avoid difficult situations. Each of these forms can be critical. Some of us might struggle with one, and that is a huge portion of our self-sabotage, or we might struggle with all three. No matter where you sit, I think it's important that we practice ways to overcome ourselves.

Here are six practices I gave for this particular day during May for the *31 Days of Power*. Apply whichever ones you need and use them so you can find your power and stop tricking yourself out of the best things that life has to offer you.

The first practice is to gain an understanding of self-sabotage. As I previously stated, a lot of times we are practicing self-sabotage and don't know it. All we know is that when something big is coming up—a great opportunity or moment—there's always something that seems to hold us back or hinder us from forward progress.

If we can identify that area, we can pinpoint some of them back to self-sabotage. It's important for us to make sure we have a clear and concise understanding of self-sabotage and its effects, which leads to the next practice of being able to overcome.

We have to get to the root cause of our sabotage. In my books, I always believe that it is better to be a step ahead of our issues than potentially being blindsided by them. I know many people right now who are aware they indulge in self-sabotage. They will claim it, let you know they do it, and giggle and laugh about it, but they haven't made any strides or steps into dealing with it and overcoming it. I don't want this for you, and I'm sure you don't want it for yourself, so we need to get to the root of the issue.

I previously mentioned three major causes for self-sabotage: fear, thinking and overthinking patterns, and not wanting to face moments of uncomfortability. Many times, the root causes are nestled in one of those or maybe all three, so we need to address our fears first. We must find out what it is we're fearful of. Is it that we've never gained the level of access or success we're about to walk into? Could it be that we've never experienced the level of vulnerability or trust in a romantic relationship, and we're simply waiting for something bad to happen?

This is how the fear factor works when we are entangled with self-sabotage. But this is also how the overthinking starts to get to us, as well.

We think ourselves out of some of the greatest opportunities. The outcome is that we feel blindsided, claiming we don't know where it came from or how it happened, but we don't accept the accountability that it started and finished with us. The same can be said about having to deal with difficult or uncomfortable things. Sometimes our fight to avoid contention can be holding us back. It doesn't mean we have to indulge in drama, but for some of us, we are afraid to consider having tough conversations with people or discuss certain topics. We don't realize when we use our voice to have hard conversations that we could have been opening doorways to freedom and healing for others. Unfortunately, it's that initial fear that will stop us. I can't tell you how many times I've done this to myself, specifically in my career over the last 10 years.

The next practice we have to put into play is learning our self-sabotaging behaviors and practices. Now that we have been able to admit that it's something we do and something we struggle with, we can try to point it out in our lives. Having a sense of understanding of our habits and ways of function can help us to do two things.

The first is to gain an ultra-sense of awareness when it's happening. The second is that it will allow us an opportunity to stop it in its tracks, which is going to be crucial when it comes to getting out of our own way as we move into these new amazing opportunities that we deserve.

I believe these last four points are going to be very helpful and shift us out of the imposter syndrome that causes us to sabotage ourselves into more of a mindset that lets us know that we deserve all of the great things that are presented before us and to us.

The next area of practice that I believe is so needed is that we change our behaviors and patterns. To do this, we need to take time to look for ways to bypass opportunities to respond in sabotaging manners. We need to lean more on the side of embracing what is being presented to us rather than embracing thoughts of being unworthy or being an imposter. This will also require us to face whatever it is that has us fearful or that causes us to overthink and think our way out of good things.

Notice what I said: This is a full change of behavior, which essentially means you have to not only think differently about yourself but also act on new thoughts that you have toward yourself.

The next step is for us to make sure we are being consistent in our small changes. In my book *The Other Side*, I write about the power of doing the small things right consistently. I think a lot of times when we talk about overcoming hardships, setbacks, or downfalls, we try to approach it in a way that sometimes has us putting too much on our plate at one time. It's almost like a person trying to go cold turkey with food choices in an attempt to make a lifestyle change. Even though being able to see a huge transformation at one time can seem inspiring, the reality is that often real transformation comes from being consistent in the small baby steps.

It's the same way when it comes to breaking the mold of our imposter syndrome and sabotaging tendencies. Don't make big changes all at once. It's easier to maintain and build on the smaller life changes. Obviously, there might be detrimental areas of sabotage that need to immediately go, so my encouragement in making small changes is to start knocking out those big bottles first.

My next point is more of an encouragement than anything else, which is that you deserve a seat at whatever table when opportunities present themselves. If it's the love you've always been looking for, that job you've worked so hard to finally get, or simply happiness in life, you are worthy of all these things. Many times, we think and live as if we don't deserve anything more than what we currently have. That fear of something greater than what we have growing up can wreck our lives in these moments of new opportunity. You deserve a seat at the table. You deserve joy, peace, happiness, and wholeness. You deserve to sit at the table with the big dogs that you looked up to. You are an equal.

A great deal of sabotage comes from the way we think. Earlier in this book, I talked about anxiety. Those anxious thoughts can be a benefactor in tricking us in major moments of advancement. Don't be fooled; you are good enough. Yes, you might be the first in your family to do something this brave and courageous or have an opportunity set before you. Maybe no one was there to give you a blueprint on how to do it before. Maybe you didn't see positive and productive romantic relationships while growing up but now find yourself in the middle of one. Please do not set yourself up for failure by believing things that are simply not true. You deserve it, you are good enough, and it is your time to reap from all of the hard work you put in before you reached this point.

The things in life you were told you weren't good enough to attain but now find yourself staring at—believe that you are good enough for that, as well. This is my final takeaway for you as we close this chapter. You are good enough.

Take time to look over today's questions and reflect on whatever speaks to you.

You are good enough!

•In what ways have you sabotaged yourself from things that you truly deserved?

•How do you want to approach your self-sabotaging habits moving forward?

Day 22

Supporting a Partner with Mental Health Issues

Supporting a partner with mental health issues is not an easy journey. As someone who has been on both sides of the coin in such relationships, I can attest to how difficult it might be for one to want to stay in the fight. Romantic relationships as a whole bring a new dynamic to a person. While there might be a lot of love and bliss, there can also be hard times. Relationships put us in positions to learn a lot about ourselves even though many times the outcome we tend to see is the finger pointed at the person we've committed ourselves to.

When you bring mental health issues into the fold of a relationship that already carries so much, it can feel overbearing for everyone involved. One personal belief I have is that even for those who have mental struggles and issues, it does not mean they don't deserve to be in a fruitful and loving romantic relationship. It can be easy to feel unworthy of having true love because of mental health struggles. I believe with a healthy balance of communication, transparency, and honesty, you can make any romantic relationship work. The same can be said for a romantic relationship that might have one person struggling with mental health.

Earlier in this book, I talked about the importance of recovery, and I stand by that. However, individuals have recovered from traumas but can still struggle from time to time. We won't be perfect, and it won't always be super clean and neat. I've seen some amazing relationships thrive and flourish with individuals with mental health issues because both parties work together to learn, heal, and thrive.

Today, my hope is to leave you with some simple things that you can do to support a romantic partner if he or she is struggling with mental health issues. Maybe this isn't for you today, but depending on the complexity of life later on, it might be something that pops up. The point I'm making is that being knowledgeable of the steps can help you become equipped if you ever find yourself in such a position.

The first thing I would encourage you to do as the individual on the helping hand is to take time to learn the symptoms. I'm specifically talking about the symptoms of whatever the mental health struggle is with the person you are with. Understanding and learning the symptoms, along with not taking their struggles personally, can help. When we are in friendships or relationships with those who struggle mentally and emotionally, it is easy to get caught in our feelings because their struggles can feel like an attack on us. Maybe it's something said or done that wasn't meant to be harmful but it came off as such, and that's how we perceived it.

As we take the time to learn symptoms, we are allowing ourselves to build a sense of maturity by being able to see the struggle and separate them from the person we love. Many times, it's easy for us to throw the two together, which will tend to become a full-on war. Learning the symptoms of their mental health issues can give an upper hand as to how we choose to respond and approach every situation that comes our way.

Next, what we can do to help is to communicate openly. Speaking truth, listening, and respecting each other's feelings while displaying good, active communication help to set a healthy foundation for the relationship. I believe that as we communicate openly, it's also important to enter communication with the mindset of love and respect.

I'll be talking about this a little more as one of the practices later on in this chapter.

Often in communication, we tend to let feelings or thoughts fester within our head, and unfortunately, by the time we let them out, they tend to come out in frustration and anger. When this happens, communication lines get crossed, and usually, no productivity comes from what is said or done. I want us to make sure we are practicing early communication and being open about our feelings. This will help in the long run to avoid unnecessary bad moments.

The next important thing for us to do as the person in the relationship who is entrusted with the struggles and heavy information is to ensure we aren't throwing our partners' struggles in their faces. It is very easy to say hurtful things by using our partners' struggles as the source. This type of action can do much damage in a relationship and has done so much damage in relationships already. We have to remember that in times like this when the person we're with lets down his or her guard and becomes vulnerable, that in itself is a gift we need to cherish. If we aren't mature enough to do so, we need to take time to evaluate ourselves and our hearts.

It's not always an intentional act when someone throws a person's struggle or area of weakness in his or her face. I've seen this happen through the heat of the moment after allowing feelings to fester without any communication. When we let things sit dormant like this, all it takes is one heated argument or discussion for everything we've been holding onto to come out in a way that can do so much damage to the relationship, the person we're with, and even ourselves. If we're going to commit ourselves to a relationship with a partner who struggles with mental health issues, we must constantly remind ourselves not to weaponize his or her struggle. This is a better time than ever, to not only reflect on it but to make the necessary changes and serve out apologies where needed.

Another thing to remember and to practice would be good listening. I'm a firm believer that good listening helps. We have tendencies to hear what we want or automatically respond. I'm urging you not to be so eager to approach these types of moments the way you normally would. Let's not listen to try to fix or to simply have a response. I believe a more effective practice would be to take in what they're telling you. As you're taking in what they're telling you, take time to contemplate and consider.

I want you to consider two things specifically. The first is to consider what they've said and fully think it through. The second part is considering how you should respond and move forward after taking the time to consider what they've said.

Good active listening can save a relationship much time and minimize the opportunity for hurt and pain to be a constant torment. For some of us, this might be a real challenge. We're used to being a fixer or we might want to get the problem out of the way so we don't have to deal with it anymore. Unfortunately, it does not work like that. When you consider what a relationship is and what it represents from a standpoint of commitment, you must be willing to commit on all levels. Sometimes, the commitment is growing past our own ways or how we've seen things done in the past that weren't productive in other romantic relationships. Let's take the time to be better and be different with our listening. The goal is to not hear what we want but to truly hear what's being said.

The next practice that can be helpful is displaying empathy and love to our partners with their mental health struggles. I believe that love truly does conquer all. For it to do so, we must learn how to empathize and be love in action. Empathy helps us to be able to look at situations beyond our own understanding. Just because we haven't had the experience doesn't mean that what others are going through isn't real. I see this being a great help in a romantic relationship. Learning to empathize with our partner and walk with him or her is a huge part of the healing process. When you think about what love is, you can't have love without empathy. Be able to be selfless enough to learn and understand the growth of something bigger than yourself. We need to ensure that our display of love and empathy are greater in those times when our significant other is struggling.

The next practice I would encourage for you to do is to let your timetable go. I believe it's easy for us to get caught up in how long we think something should take to change or heal. It's similar to dealing with an injury, going to see the doctor about that injury, and the doctor telling us how long it will take to recover. Unfortunately, a person's battle with mental health is not the same. Because we all have a mental health, we must remember that the opportunity for our mental health to be attacked or triggered will always be there to a certain extent, so I believe we have to keep this as a reminder for ourselves when we think it should look a certain way. There is power in learning to love someone through the ebbs and flows of his or her struggles.

The final takeaway I want to give you in helping your partner who struggles with mental health issues is to make sure you are seeking out community support. When I say "seek out community support," there are two forms. The first is having a community that can support both of you. Being able to be around other couples can be beneficial for your relationship, as well as a few close friends you know and trust. More importantly, the second form is to have community support for yourself. As much as your partner needs help, so do you. I think it's important to have good people, known by you and your partner, around you who can give you a break or encouragement when needed. Trust me; you never know how much you need community until you don't have it, so set up a system of individuals who can pour back into you, as well.

A relationship in which a partner might have mental health issues is sometimes a road less traveled, but it doesn't make this road any less worthy of the fullness of love, joy, and happiness.

Here's a quick recap for today's conversation. We must have open dialogue, honest communication, selfless love, commitment, and a strong community if we intend to support our partner through mental health issues.

Take time to look over today's questions, reflect, and answer whatever speaks to you.

• Be honest, can you see yourself being someone who would be able to support a partner with a mental health issue? If not, it's okay.

• In your opinion, what are some of the benefits for a person helping a romantic partner who might have mental health issues?

• You might have a friend who is supporting someone with a mental health issue. What are some ways you might want to support them as they help your partner?

Day 23

The Power of Community for Your Mental Health

In the previous 22 days of this book, I've referenced the power of community God knows how many times. I don't want to bore you with it; however, there is so much importance in the power of community. While I have taken a lot of time in referencing it in this chapter, I want to be intentional on why it is so important for your mental health, so we will go through the actual why and how of the need for community.

I thought it would be important to dedicate a full day to this conversation, because embracing community is not an easy task for many people. For some of us, we remain isolated, or we can just be stubborn and think that we can do it all on our own. That's the furthest thing from the truth, so my goal with this chapter is to simply give you a few things to consider to encourage you to utilize or seek community.

The first benefit to community is support. There's huge power in knowing there are people who support you. And when we know that people support us, we find a sense of safety. It feels like home a lot of times. With that support, we also feel heard and cared for more than we normally would on our own. We, as humans, are all thinkers in some capacity. Some of us take on the task of trying to think every moment and step of life through by ourselves. That can only get us so far. Having that support and community that allows us to be heard takes the weight off of our minds with everything that we might be thinking about but never speak about. Also, when we're cared for, it can change how we choose to approach every situation and our perspective on life as a whole. Even in times where a mental and emotional state might not be the best, we are still on the winning side because we have the support of our community in moments that could potentially be very dark.

One area in which I believe community provides help is with our life's purpose. There's something strong and inspiring about having people who play different roles in our lives. When this happens, those individuals help lead us to a greater sense of wholeness. I talked a little bit about this in my book *The Other Side*. The beauty of relationships within our community is that everybody serves a different purpose. Our friends in our community are all unique in their own ways. Their uniqueness adds value to areas of our lives that we may be lacking in or could use more support in. This doesn't mean that you need to have a ton of friends around you to provide every little thing, but even having a few can make a difference when it comes to perspective and opportunities to learn.

One benefit the power of community gives us is an amazing sense of belonging. The right community will give us a feeling of belonging and love. As someone who struggled early on with loneliness, I can attest to this point. When I finally started hanging around the right community, it was amazing how my mindset started to change. I didn't have to worry whether someone cared or if I was really welcome into a space. The beauty of the sense of belonging and community is that it also gives you a greater understanding of areas in groups of people who either do not deserve you or who aren't for you. Sometimes we tend to engage in community with people who do not appreciate us, see our value, or truly care about us. When you know what that sense of belonging feels like, you will also know when it doesn't.

The next takeaway point I want to give you is probably one of the most important ones but one we tend to run from a lot. This is the need for accountability that community can provide; that is, the community helps us in time of need. It is hard for us to overcome battles in our lives when we are the only ones who know about them. There are times when we need to be checked and corrected. There are struggles we live with privately that we don't need to, and having someone accountable can make a huge difference.

Now hear me out. You are capable of accomplishing great things, but capabilities can turn into victories when we have the right people to help us carry that load. I can't tell you how stubborn I've been, constantly saying I can do it on my own. And each time I tried to do it on my own, it would last for a while, but there always came a point where I fell into a trap or met my demise.

Whether it was the accountability I needed while losing weight, going through an eating disorder, or staying in a positive mindset as I tried to bounce back from my almost life-ending suicide attempt 12 years ago, the help that it provided was evident in my transformation. We must evolve beyond being capable, and the best way to do that is by having individuals who will always hold us accountable.

As you consider your community, I want to encourage you to make sure you aren't around a ton of "yes" people. You don't need individuals who will gas you up and encourage your nonsense. You want to have strong folks around you who can tell you, from a place of love, when you are wrong, as well as right. We need to hear from a perspective other than our own sometimes. While our perspective matters, it may not always be right. Understand that your support system of friends and mentors is a great sounding board and voice of reason when your need is high.

Your community doesn't have to be everybody all at once. It's about having the right people in the right position who are able to support, love, and hold you accountable when needed. I know some of you may feel you can do it on your own, but none of us were truly meant to do this thing called life on our own. When we talk about our mental health and the ways it can be triggered, we've got to understand why having people in our corner is essential.

Take time to look over the simple questions for today's conversation about community.

• Is there a community of people around you that can be helpful in your mental health?

• Have you been too shy to reach out to your community? Has embarrassment tried to show its ugly face in times where you thought about reaching out to your community?

• How do you envision community being able to help you with your mental health?

Day 24

Seven Reasons Why Suicide Isn't Your Answer

Just a few days ago, I found out that a schoolmate had taken his own life, so I'm writing today's chapter with even more intentionality.

Earlier in the book, I discussed warning signs with suicide and a few other conversations around it, but today is different. This is simply for anyone who's ever had ideations or is tormented by the thought of it. Sometimes we should remind people that their lives matter. Sometimes we need to be reminded ourselves that we have a purpose and that we're not a waste of space. Maybe you need this right now or someone you know does. Share it!

There are seven main reasons for me as to why suicide is not the answer. Take what you will from this chapter.

Before I give the seven thoughts, note that these are not only things we can use as reminders when combating suicide, but things you can keep yourself reminded of daily.

The first reason why I would argue that suicide is not the answer for you is the mere fact that you belong. I know that sometimes belonging can feel far and few in between. And it's weird because for each of us, belonging looks different. For a long time, I thought that belonging was a conversation for individuals who did not have a ton of friends, but as I've matured, I realize that even those who are surrounded by a ton of people can still feel as if they don't belong.

For some of us, we haven't found the right groups yet or the right type of support system that will affirm that sense of belonging. Because this might be the case, I believe this is a better reason than any to stay on this side and continue to learn and give life a try.

Another thought I want to leave you with is that your life has value. Coming from someone who did not see the value of his life for a good span of teen life into young adulthood, I know this to be true. Maybe you notice how other people are treated who share some of the same spaces you do and you feel as if they don't value your presence the same way. Maybe you look at yourself as being average or mediocre, but you are not. It can be hard for us to see the value we bring to the table, but I don't believe that any of us are value-less people.

I've had conversations in my other books about being able to find identity and going on the journey of learning— knowing and loving ourselves. It's on that journey where I believe we get a chance to understand our value a little more. We will get a chance to see what we bring to the table and maybe get something that we overlooked or simply just didn't give enough credit to. A lot of times, too, I think we place our value in the wrong things or think that our value should look a certain way. This kind of thinking clouds our minds and causes us to start doing things out of character.

I encourage you, as you reflect on yourself and who you are as a person, to find your value by being open to seeing even the smallest things because even the smallest things can bring some of the greatest impacts.

The next reason why I believe suicide isn't the answer is that you are not a waste of space. I've heard this from so many people I've worked with. In the midst of our frustration when individuals explain where they are in life and what they're going through, this has been a common phrase. I'm here to let you know that this is not true. You are not just taking up space or air. You are not an inconvenience, even if other people have said that to you out of their frustrations or issues. I'm simply asking that you don't start holding those words and thoughts as truth in your life because it's the furthest thing from the truth.

Reason three is that you are not a mistake. One thought that torments us a lot when we are contemplating suicide is the idea that we shouldn't have been born or that somehow we slipped through the cracks. I've even heard people talk about how they feel as if it's their mistake because this is what they were told by parents or siblings while they were growing up. I can understand how hearing something so vicious over and over again can cause people to question their self-worth and purpose, but I'm here to let you know that you are not a mistake. A perfect plan was designed with you in mind before you were even born. I believe it is worth going on the journey to figure out what the perfect plan and design are. Many times, we don't give life a try, to see the potential good that I'm referencing right now.

Another reason I believe suicide is not your answer is that your best days are still ahead of you. I know that sometimes experiences can feel as if things are getting worse. Maybe you've been caught in a drought of bad circumstances or traumatic events. Because of this, you might be thinking back to the old days and how things used to be. I need you to know you still have greater things to accomplish and witness in the future. When we get into this idea that we've already seen our best days, we can feel as though we are okay going out. I don't want this for you. Once again, I encourage you to be bold, take a journey, and give future opportunities a try.

The next reason is the simple fact that your life matters. I know that questioning our purpose or whether we were a mistake leads us to question whether anyone would care if we disappeared. I believe it speaks to a greater issue that people face, which is knowing that the person they are matters and that if something happened to them, they would be missed. This is something I dealt with for a long time while going through my struggles and wondering if my life mattered. Loneliness has a way of tricking us into this thought.

Why have I been encouraging that concept of community so much? We can see the value a lot easier being around the right people who can keep us reminded in those moments when we need to hear it the most. This almost acts as a highlight reel of memories in those times we think we don't matter. It gives us an opportunity to consider special times with special people, and we get a chance to see just how much we matter to those around us.

The final reason I believe that suicide is not the answer for you is simply the fact that your life's purpose is greater than an early death due to suicide. You truly have a life that is worth living. With our struggles and what we see in front of us, we might not always believe this, but I want to encourage you by letting you know that you weren't created to go through life feeling miserable, going through everything you've gone through, and then dying by your own hand. That is not the case for you. I know that life is hard. People suck a lot of times, and mentally and emotionally, we get so overwhelmed we don't know how much more we can take. I understand and feel all of that, but despite that, it does not take precedence over how special you are and how needed you are.

Many times, we feel as if suicide is the only way out, but it's not. Yes, the pain we experience feels real, but there is hope for you. If you find yourself in this position, reach out to someone close to you. Even reach out to another person who may not be the closest to you but has made you feel like someone at some point. Reach out and take the risk of sharing what you're going through so you can get the help you need. And when I say "get the help you need," I don't want you to feel as if you are crazy or a lesser human being. When I say "get the help you need," I'm talking about having a safe space to release so you can heal from every battle you've gone through or might currently be going through. You will be surprised to find out who cares for you when you open up.

I believe there is so much power in opening up for both parties. On your side, it helps because it leads you down a path to pursue healing. On the other side, it helps the person who receives this information because it's a moment of perspective and also a motivating factor to help people open their eyes and pay more attention to those around them.

My final bit of encouragement for this chapter is this: Say no to suicide.

Take time to read today's questions, reflect, and answer whatever speaks to you or whatever you feel you need.

•Have you dealt with sadness and depression at such a rate that you questioned the purpose of your life?

•Have the thoughts of suicide been something you've dealt with?

•What would be helpful to make you believe that your life is worth living beyond the moment?

•How has suicide affected you or someone you know?

Day 25

Your Mental Health Through and Post-Divorce

Today's conversation won't be for everybody. I'm fine with that, but I feel it's still important to put it out there.

As we talk about simplifying conversations around mental health, I believe one of the easiest ways to do that is by connecting our mental health to real-life circumstances that could have a negative effect on it. In the last chapter, I talked about the reasons why suicide wasn't the answer. Mental health experts have made it known that divorce is a risk factor for suicide, especially for men, and even more so during a year like 2020.

Today, let's break down some of the thoughts that come with divorce. As someone who has, unfortunately, gone through a divorce, I've experienced a lot of these feelings I'll be talking about. These intrusive thoughts can start small; however, as our marriage falls apart, we see a quick mental decline. I believe if we can get a hold on some of these intrusive thoughts, we can start to gain ground on fighting back despite what we've committed ourselves to might be ending or has ended.

The first intrusive thought I want to combat is that you are somehow a failure. To that, I say: You are not a failure.

Failed marriages can easily cause us to label our entire lives as failures, and this is furthest from the truth. We tend to reflect on the wrong things and look at everything that did not go well in our lives before our marriage. Sometimes we tell ourselves lies, such as that failure is all we know or that we'll never be able to get anything right or hold onto anything meaningful. These are all things that caused us to feel as if we are somehow failures because of failed marriages. I need you to know that this is not the truth. You can pick yourself back up, along with the pieces, when it comes to understanding where the marriage failed, without proclaiming yourself to be a failure.

Confusion is the next thing I believe we need to tackle. For many of us, confusion is a common feeling associated with divorce. In moments of confusion, we will create thoughts and scenarios. I don't believe that confusion starts at the point of divorce, either. Typically, there is a level of buildup that exists already. You start to experience a lot of the confusion when you notice your marriage spiraling out of control or going downhill. With that said, however, that same confusion continues to grow by the time we reach the point of divorce.

Quite often, the things we are creating do not even exist. However, if we allow ourselves to be controlled because of what we've imagined, we can create ugly things from that post-divorce. This is why I believe we've got to take a step back and use that logical thinking that was discussed earlier on in this book. We must be cautious in what we choose to believe about ourselves after divorce.

Another common area of struggle that we have in divorce that can lead to emotional damage is embarrassment. Divorce can easily open the door that causes you to question what others are thinking about you and your situation once it goes public. Public embarrassment hurts. We might be able to handle ourselves well in the moment of public embarrassment, but once we are on our own and have time to sit and think about what happened, it can be some of the worst torments.

Embarrassment was at the top of my list. Instantly having to explain or trying to avoid conversations with people when they ask about the divorce can be draining. That embarrassment has a way of staying latched to us a lot longer than we would like. Here's my encouragement for you: I know there are numerous thoughts that can lead to embarrassment, but we've got to be able to break down what it is that embarrasses us.

I think it's also safe to say that we've got to consider who we think we're an embarrassment to. This thought will be helpful when it comes to being able to retrain thoughts that could lead to depression and, as well, anxiety that exists from embarrassment. The reason I say this is because as we break down embarrassment, we realize a lot of it rests in our minds. Will people have their opinions about us or our situations? Absolutely. But others aren't living your situation, so be careful not to allow their thoughts and opinions to eat away at your psyche. You know those who genuinely want to help, and I'm pretty sure you can discern those who are nosy. Categorize people accordingly so you don't have to constantly go through these types of thoughts.

The feeling of time wasted is a common one for people who've gone through a divorce, even romantic relationships in general. More so when you consider marriage and the things that were done to create the marriage. You might find yourself thinking back on all of the money spent on the wedding, all of the items you share in the same name, and trying to figure out life on your own after being codependent. Divorce can make you feel as if you have wasted time that you will never get back. I think we can be hopeful by shifting our focus to the lessons that can be learned.

Lessons come in different forms during this process. I believe the first lesson we can learn is about ourselves during this time. It takes two to tango, which means you play a part in the marriage, as well. Combine that with the fact that none of us are perfect beings and you will see there are things you can learn about yourself from your time during the marriage that can help you grow as you move forward. It is hard to see the not-so-good parts of ourselves. We all struggle to see our flaws, but that is where a good amount of our maturity and growth will develop.

I mention this being important for the areas in moving forward, which leads me to my next point. Many people struggle after divorce with the question, "Will I ever find real love?" For some, it's almost like this overwhelming sense of hopelessness when it comes to believing that the right love exists.

I want to let you know that true love does exist and you are deserving of that love. The idea of being damaged goods is a common thought for many. When we consider how much time we think we've wasted and the experiences we've had in what we consider a failed space, it is easy for us to get into a rhythm of thinking that dysfunctional romance is all we will ever be good at. That's not true.

I believe it is important to resort back to what I mentioned in an earlier chapter. Take time to heal and gain an understanding of areas of improvement you would like to make. Also, you can use this time to figure out what it is that you truly need that will help you in a romantic relationship. Over time, you'll find you have grown, not only in your thoughts but also in your decision-making to minimize the possibility of embracing love from a person who might not be right for you.

The next point has to do with an earlier conversation, as well. I previously mentioned in this book about taking time to identify whether we are the toxic person. We talked about divorce being one of the things that tends to be filled with toxicity. This is not to say that all divorces are super toxic; however, the opportunity to practice it exists, so my encouragement for you in the space is to practice integrity. I know how anger and bitterness linger in our minds. They give us an opportunity to gossip about the person we are no longer with or to share intimate details that others shouldn't know. The opportunity to be petty may be appealing to cause greater damage to the other person, but don't take the bait.

My challenge is for you to be better. Even if you feel like the person wasn't good to you, I need you to understand that every time you take on that opportunity to embrace being toxic, you are also hurting yourself by dragging the relationship out even more. Please remember to check yourself often because you don't want to become the very thing that hurt you.

As we get ready to finish today's reading, I don't want to leave without a final thought. No one marries to get divorced. Also, there isn't a perfect layout on how to handle a divorce. A lot of times, people try to figure this out on the fly while also being torn down emotionally in the process. That anxiety hits differently when you know the downfall is inevitable. With that being said, we've got to determine what we're feeling when we're feeling it. We want to ensure that we stay connected to a few friends or family members during moments like this, as well. When divorce happens, it becomes easy for people to isolate themselves from everyone, which is not helpful at all. This is where we get into the greater conversations of suicide rates. I want you to know that you are not a failure, and even though the marriage didn't work, it doesn't mean you aren't worthy of a better life moving forward.

Take time to look over today's questions and reflect on whatever you need.

•As I stated, this chapter won't be for everybody, but if divorce is something you've experienced, how has it affected you?

•What are some ways you would like to pick up the pieces moving forward after a divorce?

Day 26

Overcoming Fear

Fear is a real battle. It can show itself in different forms. For some of us, we might have a phobia that causes fear, such as spiders or clowns. Others might be fearful when it comes to scary movies or theme park rides. These experiences that lead to fear are all legitimate, but these are not the fears I'm referring to in this chapter.

When I talk about the real battle of fear that so many of us go through, it usually comes from a deeper internal space. For some, they believe that all it takes is not to be scared anymore. However, that is not the case when we talk about overcoming fear that is connected to our experiences. For many of us, our fears are connected to past traumas or current traumas. The things that have us fearful are legitimate because we've had to see them firsthand and it seems as if whatever it was that caused the fear still has control over our lives.

No matter what the cause or source of our fear, one thing I believe holds true is that when fear goes unaddressed it can lead to certain mental health issues. Our fear can give power to the likes of anxiety, doubt, and even depression.

As we dive into today's reading, I want to focus in and help you learn how to get a hold on whatever it is that has you fearful, that might cause you to stumble or cripple you. These are only a few of the practices to overcome, and they are powerful tools.

Here are a few tips for overcoming fear:

The first thing I encourage you to do when we talk about overcoming your fear is to identify your fear. When you identify your fear, you can put a name to it. A quote I've heard that I frequently use is "Name it to tame it." And that's what I want to encourage you to do when you take the time to identify your fear.

For some of us, it is a lot easier to know exactly what it is that has us fearful and why it has us fearful. But for others, it will not be that easy. Sometimes our fear is rooted in issues that we have overlooked or even swept under the rug, so when I talk about being able to identify your fear, it will come with a good amount of soul-searching. More importantly, it will also come with a good amount of honesty with yourself. Pride and ego have such a way of causing us to put up walls and making statements about being unbothered or not fearful. For the sake of your mental health and your healing, I encourage you to let down those walls so you can effectively move forward. It's okay to identify the thing that has you fearful because doing it will give you the upper hand in the long run and you can live in truth when you say you aren't scared or fearful of certain things.

The next step I want you to embrace is taking the time to understand your fear after you have identified it. Once you put a name to your fear, you can start the process of understanding how the things that have you fearful function in your personal life. A lot of times, the things we are fearful of tend to run in cycles or patterns. When we pay greater attention to the patterns and cycles, we are learning how those cycles and patterns work against us. As we learn, we can overcome these cycles with strategies of our own. When we take the time to understand what causes our fear, we also have an idea of how our fears can connect to other things that we have yet to engage.

To have an understanding of what causes fear, we must educate ourselves on what we fear. This is our next point. The easiest way to understand your fear is by being knowledgeable of it. It's common that we tend to fear the unknown, so my encouragement for you is to make it known. As you make it known, you can make correlations with the fear that you've been crippled by and have a deeper level of understanding of how it currently shapes your approach to life.

I understand that the idea of getting close to the things you fear feels weird. For some, it might make you feel like closing the door and running away from it. Others might think that getting this close will cause you to be more fearful. Neither of these is true. What it's doing is allowing you an opportunity to look your fear in the face and shrink it back down to size.

It's kind of like the closing scene from the movie *It Chapter 2*. The main characters in the group known as the losers club had to go underground and stand face-to-face with the otherworldly being that had been torturing them since they were kids. Twenty-seven years later, as adults, they were still afraid of him and his antics. But this one particular scene brings to life what I'm telling you now. The character Pennywise is doing all he can to remain in control and power. However, the loser club realizes that he is only as powerful as their fear of him, so they start to call out all of the facades that he has hidden behind to use as fear tactics against them. Doing this, they turned a 50-foot mutated clown spider into a tiny clown dying from the very fear he tried to use against others. It was through their words and beliefs about how powerless over what they feared was that caused the fear to shrink. It's the same way for you and me and everyone else who deals with fear. We must analyze and break down where the power comes from within what we fear.

The next thing I encourage you to do is to change your lens. When I say "change your lens," I'm talking about the way you choose to look at your life and everything within

155

it moving forward. Now that you know the ins and outs as to what it is you fear, it's time to create a new vision. Changing the lens will help you as you approach new scenarios and experiences that might look similar to what you have feared in the past.

This leads me to the next point, which is to learn the true strength of what you fear. You can do this by asking yourself a few questions or figuring out the worst that could happen.

How big is the thing I'm afraid of? When you ask questions related to the things you are afraid of, it can help to bring perspective. This is how we can minimize what seems so big in our lives.

The final thing I encourage you to do is to ask for help. You are not the first person to deal with whatever it is that has you fearful even though you might think you are. You don't have to try to fight this thing on your own. Learn from someone who has overcome the very thing that stares you in the face. Some people carry knowledge and wisdom and are willing to help. With that being said, I also want to make sure you know that you don't have to listen to that voice in your head that may be telling you that you are a burden or that you will be a burden if you open up to talk to someone. You are not a burden. This kind of thinking can easily cause us to stay closed off and not talk about what it is we're feeling or going through. It will also act as a doorkeeper to keep the door of healing and overcoming closed.

Take time to look over today's questions and consider how you want to approach overcoming things that might lead to fear in your life.

•Has fear ever tormented you?

•What are some fears you would like to overcome so that you can live a better life?

•How do you envision yourself overcoming those fears?

•How has fear affected your approach to life and your mental health?

Day 27

Men: Their Emotions and Mental Health

With constant changes in our world around conversations with mental health, I felt that this day was an important one during my journey through *31 Days of Power*. This isn't a conversation that is had as much as it could be; however, I have noticed there's been a lot more intent behind helping others to deal with their emotions. We have grown up with so many stereotypes and myths about men being able to show emotion. Typically, it's reserved for the death of someone special or a sporting event we might've been a part of. We've been conditioned to not show emotion when we have certain feelings.

I went through this journey for the longest time, thinking that all I needed was to man up and everything would be okay. I was told that crying was a sign of weakness for a man. There's been too many ridiculous labels and titles placed on men for simply being human.

No matter how manly we are, it does not take away from the fact that we are still human. We are flawed and imperfect. Emotions are normal and deserve to be cared for and investigated into even if you are a man or know a man or in community with other men.

Today, I want to go over some unpopular facts about men and emotions. For the male readers, I hope you can take what you need from this book to heal and be reminded that your emotions are okay. My second hope for those of you in community with other men or with a special man in your life is that you keep these as solid reminders. I say this because sometimes there are unconscious moments when men might try to open up and be vulnerable, and it is not always received well. Essentially, I'm asking that we take the time to pay more attention and be available.

The first unpopular fact I want to bring to the table is that men don't have to live detached. For so long, men have traditionally been raised to remain detached from emotions and vulnerability. My encouragement is for you to take time to learn to embrace your emotions fully and reach the point where you can see that there's strength in your vulnerability. You do yourself more harm and damage by keeping these feelings bottled up inside.

This is something I did for so long, and it led me to a depressed and suicidal lifestyle. I felt I couldn't talk to anyone or that if I did, I'd be labeled or misjudged, so I dealt with it on my own. If you've read any of my other books or heard my story, you know that approach led to the final suicide attempt that almost took my life.

Living detached from your emotions is unhealthy. Mentally, it might make you feel as if you're strong because you don't have to talk about it and you just "deal with" it. But if we can be honest, many times we're not dealing with it; we're taking blows from life and feeling all of what we stored away or swept under the rug and think that's it. But that's not the reality. What's really happening is that every time we store some form of hurt or pain or allow it to build and grow, after a while we can't fit in anymore and we will explode. As men, we have to understand that we cannot find wholeness while being detached. We won't be able to find true healing from anything while being detached.

The next truth is that your feelings don't make you soft. As I stated already, you are human, and as a human, you aren't exempt from having feelings. You aren't exempt from feeling at all. You're not a robot or some kind of machine. It's in your DNA, and it's normal. You are a human being that has been created to be relational and emotional. You're not soft because you choose to learn more about what it is that you're feeling or take the time to admit that you have feelings. In my opinion, true strength comes from being honest in having feelings and addressing what we feel. It takes true strength to be able to welcome others into our emotional space.

The next idea I want to combat is the concept of you've got to man up. I've hated this term for so long. I heard it when I played sports and while having conversations with men. I even heard it in moments of high emotions, like arguments. It's become a part of our culture.

Here's my thought about it. Those man-up moments can lead to breakdowns in your personal life. When we take the man-up approach, we normally aren't addressing our pains, traumas, or emotions. When we ignore these feelings, we suppress them. In those times of suppression, whether we realize it or not, we're making room for those feelings to lead to major issues later on.

I remember growing up and hearing the term "man up" and every time I did, it usually was a thing of "stop crying" or "get it together." Truth be told, we were only getting it together for that moment. Whatever it was we dealt with before we were told to man up is still there, and it is completely unaddressed inside of us.

I believe it's important for us to realize the damage that the concept of "manning up" can cause, specifically when we are told to man up without an understanding as to what it is we're struggling with. Don't do yourself a disservice by practicing this concept, ignoring your emotions and having to deal with a future of breakdowns later on.

I want to encourage by letting you know that it's okay to let your ego go. I know this is not popular, but it's the truth. We were lied to. For so long, we were told that having feelings is feminine, so we carry an ego sometimes that aligns with this same thought process. We don't always realize we're hurting ourselves by keeping this mindset. As men, we carry a ton of pride and ego, but I don't think we realize that we carry it unnecessarily. That ego doesn't help us one bit in being able to be a healed and healthy individual. A lot of times, that ego becomes a façade that we hide behind and never have to truly discuss what we're going through.

The final unpopular fact I'm leaving you with is that, as men, you deserve to be loved and appreciated. More importantly, you deserve to be able to embrace that love and appreciation and all of the feelings that come with it. If we don't talk about our mental health and everything going on within, we won't be able to truly thrive in it if we're not embracing love and help from others. Whether through friendships, romantic relationships, or family, you need love to thrive and be healthy. I want you to know that it is okay to love and be loved. You are more of a man for acknowledging your feelings and being productive and nurturing them for a better overall mental health.

As I write this, Covid-19 is running rampant. During times like this, life seems to change daily, and one of the big points of conversation has been how suicide numbers in men are rising. I believe it's in these moments when men can be proactive with their mental health and feelings so that we can avoid outcomes such as suicide. I know it's not popular, but it is powerful. It's time for you to relearn everything you were taught about your emotions and feelings.

Take time to look over today's questions and concentrate on whatever speaks to you.

•Have you been taught that emotions in a man are wrong?

•Has what you've been taught caused you to look differently at men who express emotions?

•How do you want to better support men in your life when it comes to burying emotions?

•What are some myths you would like to leave in the past when it comes to your emotions as a man?

Day 28

Mental Health Benefits of Physical Activity

I can't stress enough the importance of physical activity when finding ways to champion our mental health. For me, physical activity helped out so much. Earlier in the book, I talked about how different forms of movements can help us in numerous and varied ways, but with this chapter, I want to take it a step further.

It's not just about basic movement but, rather, how exercise and other physical activities can be a huge benefit to our mental health. For the longest time, I was always of the mindset that physical activity would be a big help for me as far as looking good in clothing. As someone who has lost an entire person in body weight—170 pounds, to be exact—physical activity has shown itself to be more beneficial for my mind and my emotions in the last few years.

In today's reading, I want to talk to you about some proven health benefits of physical activity. A few of these have been personal experiences, and I believe wholeheartedly in them. The best part about being physically active for the sake of a better mental health is that we have nothing to prove to anyone. When we talk about physical activity that usually focuses on a form of exercise, it can be easy to get caught up on what we can't do or haven't previously done physically.

My encouragement here is to make sure you find something that works for you when it comes to your physical activities. I'm not asking you to go to the gym and lift every weight possible or to become the king or queen of cardio. I'm simply saying that every little bit you do to help yourself physically will prove itself to be of great benefit to your mental and emotional health, whether things are good or bad.

Here are my top mental health benefits from cultivating a physically active lifestyle:

The first is that physical activity has been proven to be a great stress reliever. Working out can help manage physical and mental stress that may have built up from negative experiences or current circumstances.

Earlier, I mentioned how stress is one of the leading killers amongst people. Whether we believe it or not, we tend to walk around holding in a lot of stress. Typically, stress isn't showing itself right away, but over an extended period, it makes itself known in different forms. It can come through actual physical ailments or complete burnout to the point where we feel we cannot function. It's important for us to make sure we are engaging in physical activity as it will help to pull back on the stress that stays with us and causes us to feel suffocated. I believe it can also help us to not respond to things because of our stress, which is common when we find ourselves stressed out with whatever life presents us.

The next benefit of physical activity is that it helps to provide for our mental and emotional health, and it can prevent mental declines and help to keep our memory sharp. Studies have proven that physical activity boosts our creativity and mental energy. It's almost like that adage "If you don't use it, you lose it." This works for us physically and mentally. For instance, if we usually work out but stop for any length of time, it will show that we haven't been as active once we get back into it. We might need to build our stamina back up or we might need to get our strength back up.

The same can be said about our brain and its daily functions. When we engage in physical activity, it forces us to use our minds to complete whatever the physical task is. This is how it keeps us sharp. Our physical and mental health are so much more connected than we give them credit.

Because our mental and physical health are connected, it's important to make sure we give time and attention to both. There's something to be said about being in tune with yourself to this degree that can cause you to be successful in your overall health.

The next important benefit to remember is that physical activity helps with anxiety and depression. Exercise releases endorphins, which are natural chemicals in our body that create feelings of happiness. Physical activity is a real mood changer. Lots of times when we engage in physical activity, our focus has to be on whatever task we are presented with. This is great because for many of us, before engaging in that activity, our mind might've been on a stressed-out situation that we had yet to come to grips with. It could be something as simple as a comment that got under your skin on social media or a conversation that turns you upside-down. When we engage in physical activity, we are able to get our minds off of the thing that caused us to stress out more or become frustrated. Even if for a few hours, having that time away from the problem and clear our minds helps us to re-approach the situation with better perspective and clarity.

Physical activity has also proven to be helpful for people in addiction recovery. Essentially, the activity helps to distract us from our addictions, even if for a short time. But what if, in those small baby steps, we can start learning to do it consistently? If done consistently, it can help us to de-prioritize the yearning for addiction.

This reminds me of a chapter in my book *Between the Dream*, called "Starve the Beast." This was my overall concept when creating this chapter. If we can learn to stop our beasts, whatever they might be, for a decent amount of time, we have essentially stripped away its power and control. The starvation of an addiction can lead to a doorway of healing, and this can be produced by our intentionality with a little bit of physical activity each day.

Physical activity can also help to increase our self-esteem. There is a great sense of accomplishment and completion when we engage in physical activity. The more consistent we become within physical activity, the more consistent those moments of accomplishment and completion add up. This speaks to the fact that we have started to re-prioritize positive healing methods over negative areas that have more control over us. I believe that there's also something to be said about the way we respond to our feelings. When we feel accomplished, we start to live that feeling out a lot more. This can have a major positive effect on our personal lives and how we choose to approach life overall. These accomplishments can lead to a confidence boost that becomes habitual in our daily lives.

A great benefit that comes from physical activity is that it helps to improve our sleep. Physical activity increases our body temperature, which has been known to have a calming effect on our minds. A calming effect is important because it tires us out. For a lot of us who struggle mentally or emotionally, we might struggle sleeping because our minds never seem to shut down. We find ourselves in a constant state of overthinking. Maybe we're worried about the day to come, the work ahead, or the normal uncertainties that come with day-to-day living. Being engaged in physical activity can help us be tired enough to want to sleep once the day is over. We won't have the same level of energy to give to the things that normally keep us up because we have given so much of it to whatever physical activity we chose.

No matter what your choice of physical activity is, I simply want to encourage you to engage in it fully and give it a chance by being consistent with it for a few weeks. I say this because this will not be an overnight transformation. Seeing major results will take more time than we tend to want to put out, so I'm mentioning this as a reminder for you to embrace consistency and longevity. This physical activity component is not about a look or having the greatest physique. It's about providing your body with an opportunity to connect with your brain for optimal usage and functionality for better mental health.

•What are some small physical activities you can start today that you feel you would be comfortable with?

•What are some of your fears when it comes to engaging in physical activity?

•If you've been engaging in physical activities, what are some new physical activities you would be willing to implement to better help your mental health?

Day 29

Racial Trauma: Its Effects and What
You Can Do to Help!
(BIPOC Black/Indigenous/People of Color)

The year 2020 has exposed so much, specifically around conversations of race, not only in America but around the world. Seeing more black, indigenous, or persons of color murdered on camera by regular everyday civilians has heightened this year. Couple that with body camera audio or audio from other encounters to find the incidents were racially charged, and it's easy to have a disaster.

I can't speak for the experience of anyone else, but I can speak from my experience as a black man in America who has dealt with his fair share of bias, ignorance, and flat-out racism. Racism even as far back to when I was three years old at the Gurnee Mills Mall not too far from the Six Flags Great America outside of Chicago. I remember it more and more the older I get. I was called a nigger by a middle-aged white man who got upset once he realized his daughter and I were playing together in one of the play areas. I knew something was wrong with what he said once I saw the response on my mother's face, but obviously, being so young at the time, I couldn't put two and two together.

I've dealt with my fair share of questioning as to how I could afford a nice vehicle or live in nice areas—as if I didn't work for my money as everyone else. I've even noticed I've had to be mindful of my "code switching" to talk certain ways when working with different groups or clients. Even with the changes that Covid-19 has brought, I'm noticing how racism plays a part in my daily living in those areas, as well. While I could go on and on about racism itself, that's not my focus and goal with today's reading. What I want to focus on is racial trauma—its effects and things we can do to help eradicate it and become better human beings.

Have you experienced racism or has someone close to you? Maybe you've never experienced it and don't necessarily believe it exists. No matter your answers, I believe this chapter has something for every person, so I ask that you approach this with an open mind and an open heart. Just because my struggle isn't yours, doesn't mean it doesn't exist.

Racism, bias, and bigotry are all forms of trauma. With that being said, we must know that this can have a huge effect on someone's mental and emotional health. No matter how big or small the occurrence, the fact remains that this is now an emotional burden that someone has to carry. We might not be able to see the lingering effects, but we have to understand that, just like any other form of trauma that can affect our mental health, moments like these are the same for the person on the receiving end.

This brings me to the first point I want to give when it comes to the effects of racial trauma, which is that it produces an immense amount of pain. The stories, images, and videos that might be new to some are all-too-familiar for BIPOC. Not only are they common in today's marginalized groups, but they hurt every time we see them. While we might not be affected by it, there is still that stinging sensation that brings about pain every time something unfortunate like this happens.

That is because it's a real trigger. This is the second point I want to give you. Racial traumas can trigger and link us back to our personal traumatic experiences of racism, whether big or small. After all, it is trauma. Just because it's racism at the helm doesn't take away from the fact that since it is a form of trauma it can and will have the same effects that any other form of trauma would in our lives.

One of the unfortunate parts when it comes to this particular battle, though, is the fact that occurrences of racism are so common that it's almost as if we never get a chance to pick up ourselves from the last occurrence, which leads to my next point.

Racial trauma can feel like a hopeless, never-ending experience. I believe this is because of several different reasons. The first is that we have the initial experiences within our own lives. The next is that we relive those experiences while seeing instances of racism being recorded more and more, and then we take it to a personal level. It can feel never-ending because on a daily basis we might have to deal with micro-aggressions within our workspaces or friends' settings. We might find ourselves dealing with dismissiveness when we do decide to share an incident or pain from said experience. It can also come through acts of hatred or bias while simply being out and enjoying ourselves.

The reality is that these experiences happen every day and never seem to slow down. Imagine your anxiety or depression constantly beating you down and never letting up. This is how it feels for BIPOC.

These situations can be overwhelming. With the current racial climate that has taken place, I've noticed that a lot of people who might not identify as black, indigenous, or a person of color have been asking what they can do to help. Obviously, we have people standing on the front lines as allies, but I would like to take it a step further. With me being a super relational individual and understanding the power of community, I believe there are things we can do with the people around us to help when it comes to the mental health of our friends who go through these circumstances.

The first takeaway that I believe is so important to remember is that it's not just actions or words; it's an entire system. You might've heard the term "systemic racism" used at some point during this year of 2020, what with all of the racial injustices that have taken place.

I believe that this is an important point to remember because as we continuously see and learn, we realize that racism is deep and that it is systemic. This system was not one that was created to benefit the people that it was created to oppress. I believe that as we make forward progress in wanting to help, it's important for us to identify the systems and those that might be controlling these systems.

My next thought is this: We don't want to repeat history. We want to heal. Maybe you've seen a meme or post shared around social media from one of your friends who is black, indigenous, or a person of color stating how tired they are. Remember this! Because it is very true and important. BIPOCs are tired, not just physically but emotionally and mentally. Our spirits are tired. Just like everybody else, we want love and healing. We deserve love and healing. As individuals who might want to help in this cause, one way we can do that is to be a carrier of healing. I don't want to put limitations on what that looks like, but we can approach our conversations and everything else that we do from the mindset of carrying healing for someone we know who might need it.

This leads to another one of the points, which is not to be just an ally but learn to become family. These attempts to be more intentional and walk side-by-side with someone who doesn't look like you will be tough. It will happen through tough conversations. I encourage you not to be afraid to have those tough conversations. You may have to ask ignorant questions, have uncomfortable conversations, and have heart checks from time to time. I know how easy it can be to want to steer clear of having the tough talks and seeing things from a different lens, but I truly believe you can help in healing and bringing about a deeper bond that will create that feeling of family even with those who don't look like you or come from the same background.

We've should remember that these wounds of racial trauma stay fresh because the scab is constantly being peeled back with new actions, so healing doesn't get a chance to take place as much as we like to think it does. I strongly believe that we are better together as a healed and whole community. I'm talking about true community, not just the look of it but the intentionality that comes with it. We need to get past ourselves, to sit down and learn from and grow with current friends or people we haven't given a chance to know on that deeper level. Believe it or not, these types of small actions can help the mental health of your friends of color more than you know.

I believe there's something to be said about having people who don't look like us take the time to listen and understand an experience different from their own. Listening and learning have helped me not to become closed off and close-minded or categorizing every person biased or racist who doesn't look like me.

Let's learn how to heal together through all of this.

Please look over today's questions and take time to truly reflect when it comes to your life, experiences, and the lives of those you are in community with, those with whom you haven't taken the time to dive deeper into life. We are truly better together.

•Have you experienced racism in your life?

•Has someone you are connected to experienced racism in his or her life, and what has that done to them?

•If you don't have an answer to that last question, would you be willing to ask them and learn from them?

•What ways would you be willing to learn to advocate and help someone struggling within the realms of racism who looks different from you?

Day 30

Intentional Acts of Kindness to Encourage Others

As I was finishing up the *31 Days of Power* series during May 2020, I wanted to close the month out with some reflective thoughts. I felt this urge to keep everyone reminded that as we read through these different conversations and circumstances, which can affect our mental health, it's also equally important we remember the part we play in the day-to-day lives of people we encounter. This led me to the idea of putting together simple intentional acts of kindness to keep others around us encouraged. I want to do the same thing here as we get ready to close out these last two days.

I understand how kind gestures or acts of kindness can seem rare in today's age. With so many ugly things taking place in this world, it can be hard to believe that the light we put out will have any kind of substantial impact on the darkness. I don't want you to give up or lose hope. I know the same can be said about trying to be present or helping people who might be going through some type of mental health battle. Many times, we feel ill-equipped or unprepared. I know many of the people I've worked with and talked to about mental health sometimes carry a mindset that they've got to be a licensed professional to help. That's not the truth. We don't need to carry a title behind us to be an individual who loves and cares for people out of the kindness of his or her heart.

The same way that I've encouraged consistency when it comes to practices that will help with mental health struggles is the same way I'm going to encourage you to be consistent in your efforts of kindness. As someone who practices this daily and gets tired, I know it might feel like a drag and that some days are better than others. But even with the rough days of putting out love and joy, you still played a significant role in creating a positive change.

Let's jump into the eight simple and effective intentional acts of kindness that will help to keep others, and maybe even yourself, encouraged.

The first intentional act is showing love, which is probably my favorite one for many reasons, mainly because I have seen how genuine, authentic love can make a difference in somebody's life. When I say showing somebody love, I don't mean simply saying "I love you" but love in action, whether this comes from a smile or a hello, or holding open the door for someone or complimenting someone. It's moments like these that we get a chance to show love in action.

With the times we're in right now in 2020 while living through a global pandemic, love in action can be doing a kind favor for your neighbor, even the one who might work your nerves the most. I want to make sure that I'm clear with that last statement: Even the people who work your nerves the most.

It is easy for us to show love to those who show it back or tend to give it; however, I've noticed that it is a lot harder for us to love those we deem to be unlovable. Because we don't know the ins and outs of a person's life, we should approach moments with those we deem unlovable with a different lens.

It can be easy for our minds to have a preconceived notion as to how we plan to treat people we have categorized as difficult or unlovable, so I want to put a huge emphasis on showing love to them, as well. This does not mean you have to lie down and let them walk all over you. I'm simply saying that whatever you do when around these types of people that you do it without allowing their issues or negativity to alter the mood inside of you.

The next simple act of kindness you can practice today is taking the time to care about and ask how those around you might be doing, whether this is an associate you see every day but don't have deep conversations with or your closest friends.

Many times, we can miss the mark of knowing how someone is truly handling life. I get that we tend to become comfortable being in contact with the people we have relationships with, and it becomes easy to automatically assume that everything is okay. But there is power in taking the time to be intentional about asking how people are doing and listening to them. There are times those who struggle with internal issues may want to say something but feel they don't want to be a burden. As a result, when you ask how someone is doing, it can be a huge opportunity for him or her to speak up and receive the help he or she yearns for.

The next act of kindness is a super simple one, and that is complimenting people you encounter daily. There is something special about nice words that go a long way in a person's day. I kid you not; I found myself doing this yesterday. I was driving down the street in my neighborhood, and saw a young black guy like myself. He was dressed to the T.

I rolled down my window and honked at him even though I didn't know him, and told him, "You're looking good, bro. Keep it up."

He smiled and yelled back, "Thank you, bro," as I drove away.

The cool part about compliments is they don't have to be difficult. You can simply spot out a color or a nice trait and say something kind about it. These make a huge difference in someone's day and can change how they approach the day moving forward. Your words bring about positivity and confidence for others.

Next up in the intentional acts of kindness is letting people know that you appreciate them. I believe this one is crucial for everyone. Whether you are a high-level executive who oversees a group of employees, romantic partners, friends, or siblings, letting the people you are around know that you appreciate them can have a huge impact. Whether we like to admit it or not, many of us struggle from time to time with believing that we are appreciated by those around us. Everyone has a different way of showing their appreciation, but we can all make our appreciation more known by verbally saying it to those we encounter when we have the chance. When it comes to appreciation, my encouragement is to let your words and actions speak together in harmony.

One cool act of kindness that I see often is when friends leave a positive comment on another friend's social media page. This can be practiced in many ways, whether it's tagging a friend under a positive post that reminded you of them, gassing them up under their latest selfie, supporting their work when they post it, or just sending a simple text letting them know that you are thinking about them and care.

Some of you are reading this and thinking, *Wow, really? Social media?* When we talk about opportune moments that can interrupt bad decisions in somebody's life, I try not to put limitations on ways that those messages can reach people. It might seem a little vague or millennial-ish, but truth be told, someone could be considering taking their own life. What happens if they open up their social media app to reflect before making that decision? Boom, your positive comment is staring them in the face. The reality is that we never know, and because we don't know, it's always safe to err on the side of caution and practice kindness.

Another great practice you can put into play is making a gratitude list to give to someone you care about. To add to an earlier point about letting people know you appreciate them, I think it's equally as important to let people know why we appreciate them. A gratitude list can be helpful because it gives a rundown of that person's great attributes. There's something to be said about being able to know specifics when it comes to those in our communities. We have people with whom we've developed bonds and with whom we have a blast, but we don't always take the time to express the specifics that makes the relationship special. This can be helpful for relationships of all types to gain an understanding of the bond they have. Awareness has the power to help us with the relationships that we prioritize.

Finally, the last act of kindness I think we can be better at is prayer. This isn't for everyone; I get that. But what I've noticed for those who tend to come from more of a faith background is that this is a common suggestion people throw out when they discover someone is struggling. My encouragement is not to say, "I'm praying for you," but take the time to pray with that person.

There's a meme spreading around social media that says, "When black people say I'm praying for you, that was the prayer." The first time I saw this, I cried in laughter because I know this to be very true. But as I've taken more time to think about it, I feel we, as a people as a whole, no matter our background or race, tend to do this. It's easy for us to say we're going to pray for someone, but we don't do it. What happens, however, if we take a few seconds to be intentional and pray with someone in that exact moment?

When you talk about the effects that something like this can have on a person and in such a positive way, the possibilities are endless. This could be another strong factor in changing the way that somebody had originally planned to approach their day, so don't be afraid to throw up a quick prayer with somebody the next time you decide to simply tell them that you'll be praying for them.

In times like the ones we are currently living in, and even when times finally improve, acts of kindness have such a way of helping the mental health of others. They can also be restorative in helping our mental health.

We hear the term "random acts of kindness." I want to challenge that notion of being random. As we move forward in our efforts to help, we can no longer be random but can be intentional. Instead of having kindness as a random act, can we make it a part of our daily living? I believe this small shift can set a new precedent in how we treat each other and how our treating each other can make for a better life.

Take time to look over today's questions and reflect however you see fit!

• Do you find acting on kindness to be hard? If so, why?

• What are some acts of kindness you would like to start making a regular practice?

• How has kindness from other people helped you?

Day 31

Grace, Pace, and Power

We've finally made it to Day 31!

I've taken some time to think about what I wanted to talk about for Day 31 because on the original *31 Days of Power* that I did via social media platforms, it was simply a recap of everything that was discussed over the first 30 days. While I could do that here, I believe you must have the tools to be able to go back to specifics when you need to.

I'm changing the flow for this final day. I'm doing that by letting you into my world a little bit when it comes to the mental health process of someone—me—who coined the name "champion" and who others look at as an expert. Many times, I don't see myself as either, but I know I have been massively effective in this field of mental health, so I took time to reflect on what it's been like putting together a 31-day mental health book.

As a kid who didn't test well when it came to reading comprehension in school, you could never have told me I'd have to put seven books together to share parts of my story in an attempt to help others.

As a result, witnessing my vision of the *31 Days of Power* come to fruition makes me happy. But, to be completely honest, it was not easy. I'm not just talking about putting this book together, but the ability to take that same comprehension that used to be a struggle and write a book on complex topics. This was tough for many different reasons.

I believe the first is that even as you put out great work, we tend, as individual experts in our fields, to still feel like an imposter or question whether the work we've done is going to have an impact on people. The next struggle was procrastination. The original *31 Days of Power* series was completed on May 31, 2020. Halfway through the month, I said I could see it being a book, but then summer arrived and Covid-19 didn't disappear like many of us thought it would, and I made excuses why I wouldn't be able to finish.

Something happened over the summer, though, that caused me to take a step back and realize this book would be completed and released at the right time. I had several conversations in one day with some of the closest people to me, and from those conversations, I found that what I thought was procrastination was something a little different. Through these conversations, I realized I had set unrealistic goals trying to get this book completed while still doing virtual speeches and helping others face-to-face during this Covid-19 era.

One of the things that can be detrimental when we place unrealistic expectations on ourselves is that we feel as if we're drowning under the pressure. For others, that sense of perfectionism kicks in, and when it happens, it steals our joy and, to a degree, our creativity.

This is what happened to me. In my excitement to share a new project, I hadn't paid enough attention to the fact that I had so many other things going on and couldn't beat myself up because I didn't reach the initial deadline.

Why am I saying this? It's because I realize that I pulled away from showing myself grace and reflection on unrealistic goals. Truthfully, I'm not the only one. Many of us do this. Because we are still, as of this writing, in the middle of a pandemic, this conversation needs to be had now. We are experiencing a form of trauma almost daily when it comes to the many changes taking place. Our sense of control and our regular flow are not normal anymore. Some of us have taken the fight or flight approach. Our brains are scattered.

Maybe you're not noticing anything from it right now, but I would encourage you to make sure you're paying attention to it a little more as we move forward. We might find ourselves in this position for a while. Many believe this will be the new norm. None of us have lived through anything like what we're experiencing. For that matter, none of us have lived through what we have yet to see in the future. Because this is the case, we should learn to show ourselves grace while also learning not to let worry and fret get the best of us.

There were times this year when I found myself taking my eye off of my work and paying more attention to the great things that other people were putting out. I worried and questioned whether what I had brewing in the pot would be of any use when it was finally completed.

This is a real struggle for many of us. But we've got to be careful not to fall into this trap for the sake of our mental health.

My main thought as we wrap up the final day of the *31 Days of Power* is that we invest time into finding our power. We can do this by remembering that even though everything around us might be chaotic, we still have the ability to show up and control how we choose to respond to every situation. We can't control the situation, but we can control ourselves in every situation. It just takes practice, and I know that it's not always easy, but it doesn't mean we aren't capable of doing so. During reflection and growth, we tend to find our strengths.

As you read through each of these days, I encourage you to be intentional about growing in finding your power in these areas. Even though everything in this book wasn't for you, for the things that were, I hope you have some measure of success in finding your power.

These 31 days have challenged me to do several things. First, I always make sure I practice what I put out and that I learn to understand my role within this field of mental health—specifically, to know my role and not feel the need to be like anyone else. It's also taught me how to stick to my plans even though they might be hard at times. Finally, it's reminded me that average people like ourselves can produce life-changing work.

I'm not sure what your specific area of struggle has been through this rough and uncertain 2020, but I do know that even with all of the struggles you've had and what you've overcome, that there's still much more inside of you that you and others need.

Please ensure you are being proactive daily with your mental health. Take the time to ask yourself questions and reflect when you need to. Also, make sure that, even in your struggles and challenges, you are not isolating yourself from your community. Don't be afraid to reach out and, if nothing else, get your feelings out in the open. It doesn't mean that every issue is going to be solved right then and there, but at least you've placed it out there. This means you've caught the ear of one or several people who care for you and want the best for you.

Finally, please remember to show yourself grace and mercy, understanding that you are only human. Let's not shoot for perfection but, rather, excellence. Even as we strive for excellence, we still have room to make mistakes, learn, and grow.

When we actively learn and grow, we are following the *Between the Dream* quote that I tend to use. The quote says: "You are not losing in life, you are not failing; you were simply between the dream."

What is between the dream, you might ask? Between the dream is the point between your present moment (where you currently are) and your promise (where you will eventually be). I like to call this area "the process." Between the dream itself is the process. When you embrace your process, you embrace your progress, and when you embrace your progress, you can walk into every promise, purpose, and plan meant for your life.

Now that you've gone through these 31 days, please continue to embrace the process that is your mental health. Every day won't be perfect, but every day you get a chance to move forward, championing your mental and emotional health and learning to live in excellence!

About the Author

Richard Taylor Jr. has created an impact over the past decade as a powerful leader and voice for people around the world. He is a graduate of Northern Illinois University and obtained his Bachelor of Arts degree in Corporate and Organizational Communication. He's the Founder of TaylorMade Empowerment, a parent company that oversees the Richard Taylor Jr. brand, publishing, and several consulting ventures for corporate clients. He is also a respected self-published author of seven published books (selling over 30,000 copies) and hosts the "Between the Dream" Podcast.

Richard has become a highly sought-after speaker who brings an empowering message of victory by creating a unique way to make the conversation of mental health easier and digestible for his audiences. He has been recognized for normalizing the conversation and helping people shift from "talking about mental health" to actually "mobilizing in their efforts toward healing and freedom." Richard's story of overcoming morbid obesity, depression, multiple suicide attempts, failing in college, and domestic abuse have struck a change within people throughout different walks of life. The impact in his interactions with audiences has been life-changing and has provided the range for him to reach, impact, and have breakthrough with over 100,000 students and professionals.

Richard's goal is to create safe spaces for difficult conversations and encourage empathy in a society that is clouded with apathy. His message breaks cultural boundaries and challenges bias social norms. Richard inspires the masses to tap into their inner potential to create the change they want to see. Over the years, he has intertwined his background and experiences into a vulnerable message of love and empathy that surpasses motivating audiences. The end goal continues to be real-life transformation.

Email: booking@richardtaylorjr.com

Website: www.RichardTaylorJr.com